Clinical Social Work Exam
Secrets Study Guide

Part 2 of 2

DEAR FUTURE EXAM SUCCESS STORY

First of all, **THANK YOU** for purchasing Mometrix study materials!

Second, congratulations! You are one of the few determined test-takers who are committed to doing whatever it takes to excel on your exam. **You have come to the right place.** We developed these study materials with one goal in mind: to deliver you the information you need in a format that's concise and easy to use.

In addition to optimizing your guide for the content of the test, we've outlined our recommended steps for breaking down the preparation process into small, attainable goals so you can make sure you stay on track.

We've also analyzed the entire test-taking process, identifying the most common pitfalls and showing how you can overcome them and be ready for any curveball the test throws you.

Standardized testing is one of the biggest obstacles on your road to success, which only increases the importance of doing well in the high-pressure, high-stakes environment of test day. Your results on this test could have a significant impact on your future, and this guide provides the information and practical advice to help you achieve your full potential on test day.

Your success is our success

We would love to hear from you! If you would like to share the story of your exam success or if you have any questions or comments in regard to our products, please contact us at **800-673-8175** or **support@mometrix.com**.

Thanks again for your business and we wish you continued success!

Sincerely,
The Mometrix Test Preparation Team

Need more help? Check out our flashcards at:
http://mometrixflashcards.com/ASWB

TABLE OF CONTENTS

Psychotherapy, Clinical Interventions, and Case Management – Continued

Group Work

SOCIAL WORK VALUES

Underlying **Values of Social Work Practice with Groups** are outlined below:

- Dignity and work of every individual.
- All people have a right and a need to realize their full potential.
- Every individual has basic rights and responsibilities.
- The social work group acts out democratic values and promotes shared decision making.
- Every individual has the right of self-determination in setting and achieving goals.
- Positive change is made possible by honest, open, and meaningful interaction.

PURPOSES AND GOALS OF GROUP PRACTICE

Group practice takes a multiple-goals perspective to solving individual and social problems and is based on the recognition that group experiences have many important functions and can be designed to achieve any or all of the following:

- Providing restorative, remedial, or rehabilitative experiences.
- Helping prevent personal and social distress or breakdown.
- Facilitating normal growth and development, especially during stressful times during the life cycle.
- Achieving greater degree of self-fulfillment and personal enhancement.
- Helping individuals become active, responsible participants in society through group associations.

ADVANTAGES OF GROUP WORK

Advantages of group work include:

- Members can help others dealing with the same issues and can identify with others in the same situation.
- Sometimes people can more easily accept help from peers than from professionals.
- Through consensual validation, members feel less violated and more reassured as they discover that their problems are similar to those of others.
- Groups give opportunities to members for experimentation and testing new social identities/roles.
- Group practice is not a replacement for individual treatment. Group work is an essential tool for many workers and can be the method of choice for some problems.
- Group practice can complement other practice techniques.

IMPORTANCE OF RELATIONSHIPS IN GROUP WORK METHODOLOGY

Establishing meaningful, effective, **relationships** is essential and its importance cannot be overemphasized. The worker will form multiple and changing relationships with individual group members, with sub-groups, and with the group as a whole. There are multiple other parties who

1

have a stake in members' experiences, such as colleagues of the worker, agency representatives, relatives, friends, and others. The worker will relate differentially to all of these.

TYPES OF SOCIAL WORK GROUPS

The different **types of social work groups** are described below:

- *Educational groups*, which focus on helping members learn new information and skills.
- *Growth groups*, which provide opportunities for members to develop deeper awareness of their own thoughts, feelings, and behavior as well as develop their individual potentialities (i.e. values clarification, consciousness-raising, etc.)
- *Therapy groups*, which are designed to help members change their behavior by learning to cope and improve personal problems and to deal with physical, psychological, or social trauma.
- *Socialization groups*, which help members learn social skills and socially accepted behaviors and help members function more effectively in the community.
- *Task groups*, which are formed to meet organizational, client, and community needs and functions.

CLOSED GROUPS

Closed groups are described below:

- Convened by social workers.
- Members begin the experience together, navigate it together, and end it together at a predetermined time (set number of sessions).
- Closed groups afford better opportunities than open groups for members to identify with each other.
- Give greater stability to the helping situation; stages of group development progress more powerfully.
- Greater amount and intensity of commitment due to same participants being counted on for their presence.

OPEN GROUPS

Open groups are described below:

- Open groups allow participants to enter and leave according to their choice.
- A continuous group can exist, depending on frequency and rate of membership changes.
- Focus shifts somewhat from the whole group process to individual members' processes.
- With membership shifts, opportunities to use group social forces to help individuals may be reduced. Group will be less cohesive, less available as a therapeutic instrument.
- Worker is kept in a highly central position throughout the life of the group, as he or she provides continuity in an open structure.

SHORT-TERM GROUPS

Short-term groups are described below:

- Short-term groups are formed around a particular theme or in order to deal with a crisis.
- Limitations of time preclude working through complex needs or adapting to a variety of themes or issues.
- The worker is in the central position in a short term group.

FORMED GROUPS

Formed groups are described below:

- Deliberately developed to support mutually agreed-upon purposes.
- Organization of group begins with realization of need for group services.
- Purpose is established by identification of common needs among individuals in an agency or worker caseload.
- Worker guided in interventions and timing by understanding of individual and interpersonal behavior related to purpose.
- It is advisable to have screening, assessment, and preparation of group members.
- Different practice requirements for voluntary and non-voluntary groups as members will respond differently to each.

STRUCTURE AND GROUP PROPERTIES

Structure is the patterned interactions, network of roles and statuses, communications, leadership, and power relationships that distinguish a group at any point in time.

Group properties are attributes that characterize a group at any point in time. They include:

- Formal vs. informal structure.
- Primary group (tight-knit family, friendship, neighbor).
- Secondary relationships (task centered).
- Open vs. closed.
- Duration of membership.
- Autonomy.
- Acceptance-rejection ties.
- Social differentiation and degrees of stratification.
- Morale, conformity, cohesion, contagion, etc.

SMALL GROUPS

SYSTEM ANALYSIS AND INTERACTIONAL THEORY OF SMALL GROUPS

The **System Analysis and Interactional Theory of Small Groups** is a broadly used framework for understanding *small groups*. In this framework, small groups are living systems that consist of interacting elements which function as a whole. In this framework, a *social system* is a structure of relationships or a set of patterned interactions. *System concepts* help maintain a focus on the whole group, and explain how a group and its sub-groups relate functionally to larger environments. This framework describes how *interaction* affects status, roles, group emotions, power and values.

SOCIAL SYSTEM CONCEPTS AND GENERAL SYSTEMS CONCEPTS

The following are **social system concepts used in the System Analysis and Interactional Theory of small group work**:

- *Boundary maintenance*: maintaining group identities and separateness
- *System linkages*: two or more elements combine to act as one
- *Equilibrium*: maintaining a balance of forces within the group

General systems concepts used in the system analysis and interactional theory of small group work are as follows:

- *Steady state*: tendency of an open system to remain constant but in continuous exchange
- *Equifinality*: final state of a system that can be reached from different initial conditions
- *Entropy*: tendency of a system to wear down and move toward disorder

SYMBOLIC INTERACTIONISM

Symbolic interactionism is explained below:

- Emphasizes the *symbolic nature* of people's relationships with others and with the external world, versus social system analysis that emphasizes form, structures, and functions.
- Group members play a part in determining their own actions by recognizing symbols and *interpreting meaning*.
- Human action is accomplished mainly through the process of *defining and interpreting situations* in which people act. The worker uses such concepts to explain how individuals interact with others, and to understand the role of the individual as the primary resource in causing change; the significance of social relationships; the importance of self-concept, identification, and role identity in group behavior; and the meanings and symbols attributed to group interactions.

GESTALT ORIENTATIONS AND FIELD THEORY

Gestalt psychology played a major part in development of **group dynamics**. Contrasting with earlier psychologies that stressed elementary sensations and associations, Gestalt theorists viewed experiences not in isolation, but as perpetually organized and part of a field comprised of a system of co-existing, interdependent factors. Group dynamics produced a plethora of **concepts and variables**: goal formation, cohesion, group identification and uniformity, mutual dependency, influences and power, cooperation and competition, and productivity. Group dynamics (or group process) provide a helpful **framework** of carefully defined and operationalized relevant group concepts.

SOCIOMETRY

Sociometry is summarized below:

- Inspired by *J. L. Moreno's* work.
- Both a *general* theory of human relations and a *specific* set of practice techniques (psychodrama, sociodrama, role playing).
- Sociometric test are devised to measure the "*affectivity*" factor in groups.
- Quality of *interpersonal attraction* in groups is a powerful force in rallying group members, creating feelings of belonging, and making groups sensitive to member needs.

COGNITIVE CONSISTENCY THEORY AND BALANCE THEORY

The basic assumption of cognitive consistency theory is that individuals need to organize their perceptions in ways that are *consistent and comfortable*. Beliefs and attitudes are not randomly distributed but rather reflect an underlying coherent system within the individual that governs conscious processes and maintains internal and psychosocial consistency.

According to balance theory, processes are balanced when they are consistent with the *individual's beliefs and perceptions*. Inconsistency causes imbalance, tensions, and stress, and leads to changing perceptions and judgments which restore consistency and balance. The group worker incorporates *varying ideas* from these orientations. Some stress the need for the group to be self-conscious, to study its own processes, emphasizing that cognition is apparent in contracting, building group consciousness, pinpointing or eliminating obstacles, and sharing data.

SOCIAL REINFORCEMENT AND EXCHANGE THEORY

The **Social Reinforcement and Exchange Theory** in regard to group work is summarized below:

- Social exchange theorists propose that members of groups are motivated to seek *profit* in their interactions with others, i.e. to maximize rewards and minimize costs.
- Analysis of interactions within groups is done in terms of a series of *exchanges or tradeoffs* group members make with each other.
- The individual member is the *primary unit of analysis*. Many of the core concepts of this theory are merely transferred to the group situation and do not further understanding of group processes.

GROUP FORMATION

ELEMENTS IN FORMATION PROCESS

The **key elements in the group formation process** include:

- The worker makes a clear and uncomplicated statement of purpose, of both the members' stakes in coming together and the agency's (and others') stakes in serving them.
- Describing the worker's part in as simple terms as possible.
- Reaching for member reaction to worker's statement of purpose. Identifying how the worker's statement connects to the members' expectations.
- The worker helps members do the work necessary to develop a working consensus about the contract.
- Recognizing goals and motivations, both manifest and latent, stated and unstated.
- Re-contracting as needed.

WORKER'S ROLE IN CONTRACTING

The **worker's role in contracting** during group formation is described below:

- Setting goals (contracting).
- Determining membership.
- Establishing initial group structures and formats.
- All three of these elements require skillful management by the worker.

GROUP MEMBER SELECTION

The **worker's process of selecting members for a group** is as follows:

- Worker explains *reasons* for meeting with group applicants.
- Worker elicits applicants' *reactions* to group participation. Worker assesses applicants' situations by engaging them in expressing their views of the situation and goals in joining the group.
- Worker determines *appropriateness* of applicants for group, accepts their rights to refuse membership, and provides orientation upon acceptance into the group.

HETEROGENEITY VS. HOMOGENEITY

Issues of **heterogeneous vs. homogenous** group formation are discussed below:

- A group ought to have sufficient homogeneity to provide stability and generate vitality.
- Groups that focus on socialization and developmental issues or on learning new tasks are more likely to be homogeneous.
- Groups that focus on disciplinary issues or deviance are more likely to be heterogeneous.
- Composition and purposes of groups are ultimately influenced or determined by agency goals.

FACILITATING THE GROUP'S WORK

The social worker's role in facilitating group process is described below:

- Promote member participation and interaction.
- Bring up real *concerns* in order to begin the work.
- Help the group keep its *focus*.
- Reinforce observance of *rules* of the group.
- Facilitate *cohesiveness* and focus the work by identifying emerging themes.
- Establish worker identity in relation to group's readiness.
- *Listen* empathically, *support* initial structure and rules of the group, and *evaluate* initial group achievements.
- Suggest *ongoing tasks or themes* for the subsequent meeting.

BEGINNING PHASE OF GROUP PROCESS

INTERVENTION SKILLS

Intervention skills of the social worker used in the beginning phase of group process are desscribed below:

- Worker must tune into the needs and concerns of the members. Member cues may be subtle and difficult to detect.
- Seeking members' commitment to participate through engagement with members.
- Worker must continually assess:
  o members' needs/concerns
  o any ambivalence/resistance to work
  o group processes
  o emerging group structures
  o individual patterns of interaction
- Facilitate the group's work.

STRESSORS

The following are stressors that the worker might experience in the beginning phase of group process:

- Anxiety regarding gaining acceptance by the group.
- Integrating group self-determination with an active leadership role.
- Fear of creating dependency and self-consciousness in group members which would deter spontaneity.
- Difficulty observing and relating to multiple interactions.
- Uncertainty about worker's own role.

MIDDLE PHASE OF GROUP PROCESS

Intervention skills of the social worker used in the middle phase of group process are described below:

- Being able to judge when work is being avoided.
- Being able to reach for opposites, ambiguities, and what is happening in the group when good and bad feelings are expressed.
- Supporting different ways in which members help each other.
- Being able to partialize larger problems into more manageable parts.
- Being able to generalize and find connections between small pieces of group expression and experience.
- Being able to facilitate purposeful communication that is invested with feelings.
- Identifying and communicating the need to work and recognizing when work is being accomplished by the group.

GROUP DEVELOPMENT

Group Development refers to group processes that *influence the progress of a group*, or any of its sub-groups, over time. Group development typically involves changing structures and group properties that alter the quality of relationships as groups achieve their goals. Understanding group development gives workers a blueprint for *interventions* that aid the group's progression toward attaining goals. A danger in using development models is in the worker's forcing the group to fit the model, rather than adapting interventions for what is occurring in the group. A complex set of *properties, structures, and ongoing processes* influence group development. Through processes that are repeated, fused with others, modified and reinforced, movement occurs.

STAGES IN LINEAR STAGE MODELS OF GROUP DEVELOPMENT

Tuckman's Five stages:

- Form
- Storm
- Norm
- Perform
- Adjourn

Boston Model (Garland, Jones, & Kolodny):

- Preaffiliation
- Power and Control
- Intimacy
- Differentiation
- Separation

Relational Model (feminist, Schiller):

- Preaffiliation
- Establishing a Relational Base
- Mutuality & Interpersonal Empathy
- Challenge & Change
- Separation & Termination

INTERVENTION AND DEVELOPMENT STAGES IN WORK WITH GROUPS

Intervention and developmental stages of the social worker in the group proccess are summarized below:

- *Power and control stage*: Consists of limit setting, clarification, use of the program.
- *Intimacy stage:* Consists of handling transference, rivalries, degree of uncovering.
- *Differentiation stages*: Consist of clarification of differential and cohesive processes, group autonomy.
- *Separation*: Consists of a focus on evaluation, handling ambivalence, incorporating new resources.

SOCIAL GOALS MODEL OF GROUP PRACTICE

The **Social Goals Model of group practice** is explained below:

- *Primary focus* is to influence a wide range of small group experiences, to facilitate members' identifying and achieving of their own goals, and to increase social consciousness and social responsibility.
- Assumes a rough unity between *involvement in social action* and *psychological health of the individual*. Early group work was concerned with immigrant socialization and emphasized principles of democratic decision making, in addition to tolerance for difference.
- *Methodology* is focused on establishing positive relationships with groups and members, using group processes in doing with the group rather than for the group, identification of common needs and group goals, stimulation of democratic group participation, and providing authentic group programs stemming from natural types of "group living."

REMEDIAL/REHABILITATIVE MODELS OF GROUP PRACTICE

Remedial/Rehabilitative Models of group practice are discussed below:

- Uses a medical model and the worker is focused primarily on *individual change.*
- Structured program activities and exercises.
- More commonly found in organizations concerned with *socialization*, such as schools, and in those concerned with treatment and social control (inpatient mental health treatment, etc.).
- Practice techniques in this model focus on *stages of treatment.*
  - **Beginning stage**: Tntake, group selection, diagnosis of each member, setting specific goals
  - **Middle stage**: Planned interventions. Worker is central figure and uses direct means to influence group and members. Worker is spokesperson for group values and emotions. Worker motivates and stimulates members to achieve goals.
  - **Ending stage**: Group members have achieved maximum gains. Worker helps clients deal with feeling about ending. Evaluation of work, possible renegotiation of contract.

RECIPROCAL INTERACTIONAL OR MEDIATING MODEL OF GROUP PRACTICE

Summarized below is the **Reciprocal Interactional or Mediating Model** of group practice:

- Worker is not called a therapist but a *mediator* and participates in a network of reciprocal relationships. Goals are developed mutually through contracting process. The interaction and insight of group members is the primary force for change in what is seen as a "mutual aid" society.

- Worker's task: Help search for *common ground* between group members and the social demands they experience, help clients in their relationships with their own *social systems*, detect and challenge *obstacles* to clients' work, and contribute *data*.
- Phases of intervention:
  - **Tuning in/preparation for entry**: Worker helps the group envision future work, but makes no diagnosis. Worker is sensitive to members' feelings.
  - **Beginnings:** Worker engages group in contracting process; group establishes clear expectations.
  - **Middle phase:** Searching for common ground, discovering/challenging obstacles, data contribution, sharing work visions, defining limits/requirements
  - **Endings**: Worker sensitive to own and members' reactions and helps members evaluate the experience and consider new beginnings

FREUDIAN/NEO-FREUDIAN APPROACH TO GROUP PRACTICE

The **Freudian/Neo-Freudian approach** to group practice is described below:

- Groups of 8-10 members.
- Interaction mainly through discussion.
- Group members explore feelings and behavior and interpret unconscious processes.
- The worker uses interpretation, dream analysis, free association, transference relations, and working through.
- This approach aims to help group members re-experience early family relationships, uncover deep-rooted feelings, and gain insight into the origins of faulty psychological development.

TAVISTICK "GROUP AS A WHOLE" GROUP-CENTERED MODELS FOR PRACTICE WITH GROUPS

The **Tavistick "Group as a Whole" Group-Centered Models** for practice with groups are explained below:

- This approach derives from Bion's work with Leaderless Groups. Bion developed analytic approaches that focused on the *group as a whole*.
- Latent group feelings are represented through the group's prevailing emotional states or *"basic assumption cultures."*
- Groups are sometimes called *S groups* (Study groups).
- Therapist is referred to as a *consultant*. The consultant does not suggest an agenda, establishes no rules/procedures, but rather acts as an observer. Major role of the consultant is to alert members to ongoing group processes and to encourage study of these processes.
- Consultant encourages members to explore their experiences as group members through *interaction*.

IRVIN YALOM'S "HERE-AND-NOW" OR PROCESS GROUPS

Described below are **Irvin Yalom's "Here-and-Now" or Process Groups**:

- Yalom stressed using clients' immediate reactions and discussing members' affective experiences in the group.
- Relatively unstructured and spontaneous sessions.
- Groups emphasize *therapeutic activities*, like imparting information, or instilling hope, universality, and altruism.

- The group can provide a *rehabilitative narrative* of primary family group development, offer socializing techniques, provide behavior models to imitate, offer interpersonal learning, and offer an example of group cohesiveness and catharsis.
- Two inpatient group methods based on the interpersonal approach are the Interactional Agenda group and Focus Groups.

MORENO'S PSYCHODRAMA GROUP THERAPY

Moreno's Psychodrama group therapy is summarized below:

- Powerful therapy for groups that uses *spontaneous drama techniques* to aid in the release of pent-up feelings, and to provide insight and catharsis to help participants develop new and more effective behaviors.
- Five *primary instruments* used are the stage, the patient or protagonist, the director or therapist, the staff of therapeutic aides or auxiliary egos, and the audience.
- Can begin with a *warm-up*. Uses an assortment of techniques such as self-presentations, interviews, interaction in the role of the self and others, soliloquies, role reversals, doubling techniques, auxiliary egos, mirroring, multiple doubles, life rehearsals, and exercises.

BEHAVIORAL GROUP THERAPIES

Behavioral group therapies are discussed below:

- Main goals: to help group members eliminate *maladaptive behaviors* and learn new behaviors that are more effective. Not focused on gaining insight into the past, but rather on current interactions with the environment.
- Among few research-based approaches.
- Worker utilizes *directive techniques*, providing information, and teaching coping skills and methods of changing behavior.
- Worker arranges *structured activities*. Primary techniques used include restructuring, systematic desensitization, implosive therapies, assertion training, aversion techniques, operant-conditioning, self-help reinforcement and support, behavioral research, coaching, modeling, feedback, and procedures for challenging and changing conditions.

CONTRACTING WORKING AGREEMENTS IN GROUP WORK

Only if group members are involved in clarifying and setting their own *personal and common group goals* can they be expected to be active participants in their own behalf. *Working agreements* consider not only worker-member relationships, but also others with a direct or indirect stake in the group's process. Examples would be agency sponsorship, collaborating staff, referral and funding sources, families, caretakers, and other interested parties in the public at large.

The following are **social workers role in contracting**:

- Setting goals (contracting).
- Determining membership.
- Establishing initial group structures and formats.
- All three of these elements require skillful management by the worker.

INFLUENCING GROUP PROCESSES IN GROUP WORK METHODOLOGY

INFLUENCING GROUP PROCESS

Influencing group process in group work methodology is discussed below:

- The worker's ability to recognize, analyze, understand, and influence *group process* is necessary and vital. The group is a system of relationships rather than a collection of individuals. This system is formed through associations with a unique and changing quality and character (this is known as group structures and processes).
- *Processes* that the worker will be dealing with include understanding group structures, value systems, group emotions, decision-making, communication/interaction, and group development (formation, movement, termination).

INDIVIDUALIZING AND EXTERNALIZING

The worker must be prepared to help *individual members* profit from their experiences in and through the group. Ultimately, what happens to group members and how they are influenced by the group's processes determines the success of any *group experience*, not how the group itself functions as an entity. The worker should give attention to helping members relate *beyond the group (externalizing)*, to encouraging active participation and involvement with others in increasingly wider spheres of social living. This should occur even when the group is relatively autonomous.

PROGRAMMING

The importance of **programming in group work methodology** is discussed below:

- The worker uses activities, discussion topics, task-centered activities, exercises, and games as a part of a *planned, conscious process* to address individual and group needs while achieving group purposes and goals.
- Programming should build on the *needs, interests, and abilities* of group members and should not necessitate a search for the unusual, esoteric, or melodramatic.
- *Social work skills* used in implementing programs include the following: Initiating and modifying program plans to respond to group interests, self-direction and responsibility, drawing creatively upon program resources in the agency and environment, and developing sequences of activities with specific long-range goals.
- Using program *activities* is an important feature of group practice.

ANALYZING GROUP PROCESSES

The following are **categories for analyzing group work**:

- Communication processes.
- Power and influence.
- Leadership.
- Group norms and values.
- Group emotion.
- Group deliberation and problem solving.

GROUP WORK WITH SERIOUSLY MENTALLY ILL CLIENTS

Group work with seriously mentally ill clients is explained below:

- Clearly defined programs that use *psychosocial rehabilitation approaches* (not psychotherapeutic).
- Focus on making each group session *productive and rewarding* to group members.
- *Themes* addressed include dealing with stigma, coping with symptoms, adjusting to medication side effects, dealing with problems (family, relationships, housing, employment, education, etc.), real/imagined complaints about mental health treatment organizations.
- Many groups in community-based settings focus on helping members learn *social skills* for individuals with limited or ineffective coping strategies.
- Mandated groups in *forensic settings* are highly structured and focus on basic topics such as respect for others, responsibility for one's behavior, or staying focused.

CHEMICAL DEPENDENCY GROUPS

Group work for chemical dependency is discussed below:

- Group work is the treatment of choice for *substance use disorder.*
- Guidelines for these groups include maintaining confidentiality, using "I" statements, speaking directly to others, never speaking for others, awareness of one's own thoughts and feelings, honesty about thoughts and feelings, taking responsibility for one's own behavior.
- Types of groups used include:
  - **Orientation groups** that give information regarding treatment philosophy/protocols.
  - **Spiritual groups** that incorporate spirituality into recovery.
  - **Relapse prevention groups** that focus on understanding and dealing with behaviors and situations that trigger relapse.
  - **AA and NA self-help groups** utilize the principles and philosophies of 12-step programs. For family and friends, Nar-Anon and Al-Anon groups provide support.

PARENT EDUCATION GROUPS

Parent education groups are described below:

- These groups are used in social agencies, hospitals and clinics.
- Often labeled as Psycho-ed groups or Parent training groups.
- Use a cognitive-behavioral approach to improve the parent-child relationship.
- Often structured to follow manuals or curricula.
- Focus is helping parents improve parent-child interactions, parent attitudes, and child behaviors.

ABUSED WOMEN'S GROUPS

Abused women groups are described below:

- Provide warm, accepting, caring environment in which members can feel secure.
- Structured for consciousness raising, dispelling false perceptions, and resource information.
- Common themes these groups explore include the use of power which derives from the freedom to choose, the need for safety, the exploration of resources, the right to protection under the law, and the need for mutual aid.

- Basic principles of these groups: respect for women, active listening and validation of members' stories, ensuring self-determination and individualization, and promoting group programs that members can use to demonstrate their own strength and achieve empowerment.
- For post-group support, groups typically seek to utilize natural supports in the community.

GROUPS FOR SPOUSE ABUSERS

Groups for spouse abusers (perpetrators of domestic violence) are explained below:

- Work with this population is typified by resistance and denial.
- Clients have difficulty processing guilt, shame, or abandonment anxiety and tend to convert these feelings into anger.
- These clients have difficulties with intimacy, trust, mutuality, and struggle with fear of abandonment and diminished self-worth.
- Mandatory group treatment is structured. It is designed to challenge male bonding that often occurs in such groups.
- Including spouses/victims in these groups is quite controversial in clinical literature.

GROUPS FOR SEX OFFENDERS

Groups for sex offenders are summarized below:

- Typically, membership in these groups is ordered by the court. No assurance of confidentiality, as workers may have to provide reports to the courts, parole officers, or other officials.
- Clients typically deny, test workers, and are often resistant.
- In groups with voluntary membership, confidentiality is extremely important, as group members often express extreme fear of exposure.
- Prominent themes include denial, victim-blaming, blaming behavior on substances, blaming behavior on uncontrollable sex drives/needs.
- Treatment emphasizes the importance of conscious control over drives/needs, regardless of their strength or if they are "natural."
- Culture of victimization strongly discouraged.

GROUPS FOR CHILDREN OF ALCOHOLICS

Groups for children of alcoholics are discussed below:

- Individuals who grow up with parents who abuse alcohol and/or drugs often learn to *distrust* others as a survival strategy. They become used to living with chaos and uncertainty and with shame and hopelessness.
- These individuals commonly experience denial, secrecy, and embarrassment.
- They may have a general sense of fearfulness, especially if they faced threats of violence, and tend to have rigid role attachment.
- *Treatment* in these groups requires careful planning, programming, and mutual aid in the form of alliances with parental figures and other related parties in order to create a healthy environment that increases the individual's safety and ability to rely on self and others.

GROUPS FOR SEXUALLY ABUSED CHILDREN

Groups for sexually abused children are summarized below:

- Group treatment typically used with child victims of sexual abuse.
- Worker must pay particular attention to her/his own attitudes toward sexuality and the sexual abuse of children.
- Important in these groups are contracting, consistent attendance, and clearly defined rules and expectations.
- Clients may display control issues and may challenge the worker's authority.
- Confidentiality is not guaranteed.
- Termination can be a particularly difficult process.
- Common themes that come up include fear, anger, guilt, depression, anxiety, inability to trust, delayed developmental/socialization skills.
- Programming can include ice breaking games, art, body drawings, letter writing, and role playing.

TERMINATION OF GROUP PROCESS

Group members' experience of termination and the worker's role in helping group members to cope with the ending of the group are discussed below:

- Group members may have feelings of loss and may desire to minimize the painful feelings they are experiencing.
- Members may experience ambivalence about ending.
- Worker will:
- Examine her/his own feelings about termination.
- Focus the group on discussing ending.
- Help individuals express their feelings of loss, relief, ambivalence, etc.
- Review achievements of the group and members.
- Help members prepare to cope with next steps.
- Assess members' and group's needs for continued services.
- Help members with transition to other services.

METHODS OF FORESTALLING OR DEALING WITH TERMINATION

The following are **group members' methods of forestalling or dealing with termination**:

- *Simple denial*—Member may forget ending, act surprised, or feel "tricked" by termination.
- *Clustering*—Physically drawing together, also called super-cohesion.
- *Regression*—Reaction can be simple-to-complex. Earlier responses reemerge, outbursts of anger, recurrence of previous conflicts, fantasies of wanting to begin again, attempts to coerce the leader to remain, etc.
- *Nihilistic flight*—Rejecting and rejection-provoking behavior.
- *Reenactment and review*—Recounting or reviewing earlier experiences in detail or actually repeating those experiences.
- *Evaluation*—Assessing meaning and worth of former experiences.
- *Positive flight*—Constructive movement toward self-weaning. Member finds new groups, etc.

PRIMARY, SECONDARY, AND TERTIARY PREVENTION

Primary prevention is intervention begun before any evidence of the onset of a problem (parent education programs are an example). **Secondary prevention is the** early detection and treatment of a problem. **Tertiary prevention is** treatment in the acute phase of a problem.

Service Delivery and Management

QUALITY ASSURANCE

Quality assurance is an aspect of quality improvement and includes all processes involved in planning and operations to ensure that care provided is of high quality. Quality assurance (AKA quality control) includes those methods used to ensure compliance and a specific level of quality in providing services or products. Quality assurance includes devising standards as well as means of ensuring compliance through guidelines, protocols, and written specifications. One of the primary goals of quality assurance is to identify and correct errors that affect outcomes. Quality assurance reviews should be carried out on an ongoing basis and reports issued so that staff members are aware of their progress in eliminating errors and working efficiently. Quality assurance units/personnel should be independent of the programs and processes they are reviewing in order to prevent bias and should use standardized and validated instruments for assessment purposes whenever possible.

BASIC FISCAL MANAGEMENT PRINCIPLES

Understanding **basic fiscal management** principles is critical in the social work environment, where the work is almost always budget driven. The operating budget may include various private, local, state, or federal grants or donations and each of those may have specific requirements for use and/or separate budgets. Expenses must not exceed income, and interventions must be paid for out of the correct budget or budget category, so appropriate record keeping and coding of services are essential. Return-on-investment must be considered and calculated for any new proposals, such as hiring of staff. With fee-for-service contracts, services and payments are usually outlined in detail and the social workers must comply with directives. With performance-based contracts, in which reimbursement is based on meeting performance measures, measures to cut expenses and improve outcomes are generally central concerns, and every intervention must be assessed accordingly, but there is more freedom in prescribing interventions.

EVALUATING AGENCY EFFECTIVENESS

FORMATIVE/SUMMATIVE EVALUATIONS

Formative evaluations, which are done while the program is in progress, must be considered as part of the design process, and the degree to which the formative evaluations will be utilized to guide or assess the process must be determined. Formative evaluations that are appropriate should be developed for each stage. For example, a policy change may be followed by a brief questionnaire asking about the effectiveness of the policy. If the evaluations are used to guide development of the rest of a program, then strict timelines for completing the evaluations and assessing results should be part of the plan.

Summative evaluations, which are done at the completion of the program, should be planned to assess outcomes. As part of the design process, it's important to determine what exactly needs to be evaluated and how best to carry out the assessment to render the needed data.

15

COST-BENEFIT AND COST-EFFECTIVE ANALYSIS

A **cost-benefit analysis** uses average cost of an event and the cost of intervention to demonstrate savings. For example, if an agency pays for 40 hours of overtime costs weekly (1.5 X hourly salary of $27 = $40 per hour), the cost would be $1620 per week or $84,240 per year. If a new hire would cost $56,160 plus benefits of $19,656 the total cost of the new hire would be $75,816 (1.35 X base salary). Cost-benefit analysis:

- The current event cost of $84,240 minus the intervention cost of $75,816 renders a cost benefit of $8424

A **cost-effective analysis** measures the effectiveness of an intervention rather than the monetary savings. For example, if the rate of pregnancies among female adolescents in a county averages 75 per 1000 and an aggressive program of education and access to birth control decreases the rate to 55 per 1000, the program resulted in 20 fewer adolescent pregnancies per 1000.

INTER-ORGANIZATIONAL RELATIONSHIPS AND SOCIAL NETWORK ANALYSIS IN COMMUNITY SETTINGS

Health care and social welfare fields often remain poorly integrated in larger community networks and systems. Social work agencies need to better coordinate and build partnerships to more fully meet the needs of their individual clients and the community at large. One **barrier to interorganizational relationships** is the allocation of resources, as funds for both health care and social services are limited. A related concern is the interpenetration of organizational boundaries, often established to preserve resources, the client base, etc. Consequently, there is often conflict within and between agencies on how best to proceed to the next level of service and who will be primarily responsible, etc. One way to overcome past divisiveness is to have shared memberships in key planning processes, by which to map the flow of care from one level to the next. Further, always central to this process is the need to enhance how different agencies communicate with one another to provide cohesiveness and continuity.

Consultation and Interdisciplinary Collaboration

LEADERSHIP VS. MANAGEMENT

Factor	Leadership	Management
Role	Encourages change and values achievements of self and others.	Maintains stability and values end-results.
Problem-solving	Facilitates decision-making and encourages innovative approaches.	Makes decisions and decides on the course of action, generally with tried-and-true approaches.
Power	Derives from personal charisma and trust of others.	Derives from position and authority granted by the organization.
Actions	Proactive, anticipating problems and taking action to prevent.	Reactive, looking for solutions to problems after they occur.
Risk taking	Willing to take risks to achieve results.	Avoids risk taking as a threat to stability.
Organizational culture	Shapes the current culture and seeks modifications.	Supports and endorses the current culture.
Resources (human)	People who follow and provide support.	Employees who are hired to serve in subordinate positions.
Focus (work)	Leading people to work more effectively.	Managing the flow of work and personnel effectively.
Goals	Focuses on long-term goals.	Focuses on short-term goals.

LEADERSHIP STYLES

Leadership styles often influence the perception of leadership values and commitment to collaboration.

Charismatic	Depends upon personal charisma to influence people, and may be very persuasive, but this type leader may engage "followers" and relate to one group rather than the organization at large, limiting effectiveness.
Bureaucratic	Follows organization rules exactly and expects everyone else to do so. This is most effective in handling cash flow or managing work in dangerous work environments. This type of leadership may engender respect but may not be conducive to change.
Autocratic	Makes decisions independently and strictly enforces rules, but team members often feel left out of process and may not be supportive. This type of leadership is most effective in crisis situations, but may have difficulty gaining commitment of staff
Consultative	Presents a decision and welcomes input and questions although decisions rarely change. This type of leadership is most effective when gaining the support of staff is critical to the success of proposed changes.
Participatory	Presents a potential decision and then makes final decision based on input from staff or teams. This type of leadership is time-consuming and may result in compromises that are not wholly satisfactory to management or staff, but this process is motivating to staff who feel their expertise is valued.
Democratic	Presents a problem and asks staff or teams to arrive at a solution although the leader usually makes the final decision. This type of leadership may delay decision-making, but staff and teams are often more committed to the solutions because of their input.
Laissez-faire (free rein)	Exerts little direct control but allows employees/ teams to make decisions with little interference. This may be effective leadership if teams are highly skilled and motivated; but, in many cases, this type of leadership is the product of poor management skills and little is accomplished because of this lack of leadership.

COP

DIFFERENCES BETWEEN COP AND OTHER FORMS OF SOCIAL WORK PRACTICE

Differences between community organization practice (COP) and other forms of social work practice are discussed below:

- COP highlights knowledge about social power, social structure, social change, and social environments.
- COP acknowledges the reciprocal process between the individual and the social environment. It seeks to influence and change the social environment as it is seen as the source and likely solution for many problems.
- In the view of COP, social problems result from structural arrangements rather than from personal inadequacies. Consequently, resource and social power reallocation leads to changes in the community and eventually in individuals.

MODELS

The different **levels of community organization practice** are:

- Locality Development
- Social Planning
- Social Action
- Social Reform

UNDERLYING ASSUMPTIONS

Assumptions that underlie **community organization practice** include:

- Members of the community want to improve their situation.
- Members of the community are able to develop the ability to resolve communal and social problems.
- Community members must participate in change efforts rather than have changes imposed on them.
- A systems approach, which considers the total community, is more effective than imposing programs on the community.
- One goal of participation in community organization initiatives involving social workers is education in democratic decision-making and promoting skills for democratic participation.
- The organizer enables members to address community problems independently, in part through their learning, analytic, strategic, and interpersonal skills.

COLLABORATIVE TACTICS, CAMPAIGN TACTICS, AND CONTEST TACTICS

Collaborative tactics Include problem solving, joint action, education, and mild persuasion. They require a perceived consensus in goals, power equality, relatively close relationships, and cooperation/sharing.

Campaign tactics include hard persuasion, political maneuvering, bargaining/negotiation, and mild coercion. They require perceived differences in goals, inequality in power, and intermediate relationships.

Contest tactics include public conflict and pressure. They require public conflict, disagreement concerning goals, uncertain power, distant or hostile relationships.

DETERMINING WHICH TACTICS TO USE

To **determine the best tactics to use in community organization**, consider the following **factors**:

- The degree of differences or commonality in the goals between the community group and the target system.
- The relative power of the target system and the community group.
- The relationship of the community group to the target system.

TASKS/GOALS

The following are tasks/goals of community organization process:

- Change public or private priorities in order to give attention to problems of inequality and social injustice.
- Promote legislative change or public funding allocation.
- Influence public opinions of social issues and problems.

- Improve community agencies/institutions in order to better satisfy needs of the community.
- Develop new ways to address community problems.
- Develop new services and coordinate existing ones.
- Improve community access to services.
- Set up new programs and services in response to new or changing needs.
- Develop the capacity of grassroots citizen groups to solve community problems and make claims on public resources for under-served communities.
- Seek justice for oppressed minorities.

VALUES

The **values of community organization practice** are discussed below:

- Working with, not for clients, and in so doing, enhancing their participatory skills.
- Developing leadership, particularly the ability to foresee and act on problems.
- Strengthening communities in order that they are better able to deal with future problems.
- Redistributing resources in order to enhance the resources of the disadvantaged.
- Planning changes in systematic and scientific ways.
- Rational problem-solving process: studying the problem, defining it, considering possible solutions, creating a plan, then implementing and evaluating the plan.
- Advancing the interests of the disadvantaged in order for them to have a voice in the process of distribution of social resources.

LOCALITY DEVELOPMENT MODEL

The **locality development model of community organization practice** is discussed below:

- Working in a neighborhood with the goal of improving the quality of community life through broad-spectrum participation at the local level.
- Is process-oriented with a purpose of helping diverse elements of the community come together to resolve common problems and improve the community.
- Tactics include consensus and capacity building. As the organization resolves smaller problems, it facilitates the solving of more complex and difficult problems.
- The worker's roles include enabler, coordinator, educator, and broker.

SOCIAL PLANNING MODEL

The **social planning model of community organization practice** is summarized below:

- Involves careful, rational study of a community's social, political, economic, and population characteristics in order to provide a basis for identifying agreed-upon problems and deciding on a range of solutions. Government organizations can be sponsors, participants, and recipients of information from social planners.
- Focus on problem solving through fact gathering, rational action, and needs assessment.
- Tactics may be consensus or conflict.
- The worker's roles include researcher, reporter, data analyst, program planner, program implementer, and facilitator.

SOCIAL ACTION MODEL

The **social action model of community organization practice** is summarized below:

- This model requires an easily identifiable target and relatively clear, explainable goals. Typically, the target is a community institution that controls and allocates funds, community resources, and power and clients are those who lack social and economic power.
- Assumption in this model is that different groups in the community have interests that are conflicting and are irreconcilable. In many cases, direct action is the only way to convince those with power to relinquish resources and power.
- Tactics include conflict, confrontation, contest, and direct action.
- The worker's roles include that of advocate, activist, and negotiator.

SOCIAL REFORM MODEL

The **social reform model of community organization practice** is summarized below:

- In collaborating with other organizations for the disadvantaged, the worker's role is to develop coalitions of various groups to pressure for change.
- This model is a mixture of social action and social planning.
- Strategies include fact gathering, publicity, lobbying, and political pressure.
- Typically, this approach is pursued by elites on behalf of disadvantaged groups.

ADMINISTRATION

Administration is described below:

- Means of managing organizations and all of their parts in order to maximize goals and have the organization succeed and grow.
- Directing all the activities of an agency.
- Organizing and bringing together all human and technical resources in order to meet the agency's goals.
- Motivating and supervising work performed by individuals and groups in order to meet agency goals.

AGENCY ADMINISTRATION, STRUCTURE, AND MANAGEMENT

All organizations should have a **mission statement** that sets forth the purpose, goals, and target service population of the organization. An **organizational structure** is then needed to pursue the delivery of services and achievement of the identified goals. An agency typically has three levels of **bureaucratic staff**: institution-wide leaders, management-level staff, and direct service providers. Typical social service agencies follow a classic Weberian bureaucratic model of organization. In a bureaucracy, leadership flows from the "top down," and tasks are rationally delegated to employees and departments best suited to achieve administrative and agency goals.

Key **characteristics of a bureaucracy** include:

- Labor divided by functions and tasks according to specialized skills or a specific focus needed.
- A hierarchical structure of authority.
- Recruitment and hiring based upon an initial review of key qualifications and technical skills.

21

- Rigid rules and procedures generally applied impartially throughout the organization and specifying employee benefits, duties, and rights.
- Activities and responsibilities that are rationally planned to achieve overarching agency goals.

RELATIONSHIPS BETWEEN ADMINISTRATORS, SUPERVISORS, AND SUPERVISEES

While all agency staff are concerned with providing quality services, **administrators** have a more external focus, while supervisors and direct service staff are focused internally. Administrators are charged with broad program planning, policy development, and ensuring agency funding, along with managing the agency's public image and community perceptions. By contrast, **supervisors** are more responsible for the implementation of policy and programs and ensuring staff adherence to those guidelines provided. New employees (during a probationary period) and those seeking licensure may engage in more formal supervision experiences. In the case of supervision for licensure, a written agreement will outline the goals, purpose, and scope of the supervision, along with meeting frequency and duration (to accrue required licensure hours), evaluations, whether or not sessions will be recorded (videotaped, etc.), and how feedback will be provided. Consultation and supervision differ, as consultation is an episodic, voluntary problem-solving process with someone having special expertise, in contrast to continuous and mandatory oversight with administrative authority.

ROLE OF ADMINISTRATORS IN AN AGENCY/ORGANIZATION

Basic **administrative functions** include:

- Human resource management: Recruiting, interviewing, hiring, and firing, as well as orienting and reassigning employees within the organization.
- Planning and delegation: Ensuring that the organization's mission, goals, objectives, and policies are in place, appropriate, and effective, and delegating necessary tasks to achieve these ends.
- Employee evaluations, reviews, and monitoring to ensure competency and efficiency.
- Advocacy: Horizontal interventions (between staff or across a department) and vertical interventions (between departments and hierarchical staff relationships to resolve conflicts and complaints.
- Conflict resolution: Acting as a mediator and a protector of the various parties involved, ensuring equitable outcomes that remain within the scope of the organization and its goals.

BOARDS OF DIRECTORS
FUNCTIONS

The **power and authority vested in a board of directors** depends upon whether they are overseeing a private or public agency. Public agencies have board members that are largely advisory or administrative, with less direct authority than those overseeing private entities. In private agencies or voluntary organizations, the board is empowered to define the general path of the agency and to control all systems and programs operating under its auspices. The board is responsible to any sources that provide monetary contributions, to the community, to the government, and to all consumers that use the agency's programs. To be successful, members of a social service agency's board must have knowledge of all operations. The function of the board is to oversee the design of policies, develop short- and long-term planning, confirm the hiring of personnel, oversee general finances and financial expenditures, deal with the public, and be accountable for the actions of the agency.

SELECTION AND COMPOSITION

The agency's mission and overall goals must be kept paramount when **choosing board members**. Members must be committed, honest, and able to invest their time and energy in the agency. Responsibilities must be discharged with personal expertise and through meaningful relationships within the community. Interpersonal skills are essential, as board members deal directly with the other members of the board, professionals at the agency, and the general public. Some boards require the representation of certain professions within the community (e.g., a banker), but all members must bring a particular expertise to the board. The agency's mission and the personal responsibilities of each board member should be understood, and a specific orientation experience should be provided to ensure this understanding. Terms are typically limited to three years, with the possibility of a second term for those making unique contributions. The terms should rotate to ensure that seasoned board members are always available.

RELATIONSHIP OF AGENCY STAFF WITH BOARD MEMBERS

The **board of directors** oversees the development of policies by agency administrators, and the staff of the agency carries out the policies as approved. The board must hold the staff accountable for the implementation of the policies, because policy operationalization may utilize a variety of potential pathways. Administration evaluates the staff, and the performance of the staff ultimately reflects on the agency, which in turn reflects on the board. Representative staff members have the right to communicate with the board about any problems they face in implementing the policies. Open lines of communication between the board and the staff ensure success in the agency. The board, administration, and staff should have a triangular relationship based on clear job descriptions that state the responsibilities of each.

SOCIAL WORK SUPERVISOR

As a middle manager, supervisors oversee direct service staff and report to administrative directors; they provide indirect client services (via direct service staff) and primarily serve the agency.

Supervisory roles include:

- *Recruitment and orientation.*
- *Management*: Delegating duties, overseeing staff work, and resolving conflicts.
- *Education, training, and staff development*: Instructing staff regarding policies and procedures, and ensuring that training is available or pursued via in-service meetings, workshops, and continuing education courses.
- *Assessment and review*: Evaluating and providing feedback regarding staff performance.
- *Support*: Helping staff resolve issues and cope with stress and promoting a healthy work environment.
- *Advocacy*: Resolving complaints and pursuing necessary support for staff.
- *Role-modeling* of quality practice, values, and ethics.
- *Program evaluator*: Ensuring that policies and procedures are effective and that staff adhere to guidelines.

POWER

Power is defined as the ability to influence others in intended ways. **Sources of power** depend on the following:

- Control of resources
- Numbers of people
- Degree of social organization

SUPERVISION AND CONSULTATION

According to section 3.01 of the *Code of Ethics of the NASW (2018):*

- Social workers who provide supervision or consultation should have the necessary knowledge and skill to supervise or consult appropriately and should do so only within their areas of knowledge and competence.
- Social workers who provide supervision or consultation are responsible for setting clear, appropriate, and culturally sensitive boundaries.
- Social workers should not engage in any dual or multiple relationships with supervisees where there is a risk of exploitation or of potential harm to the supervisee.
- Social workers who provide supervision should evaluate supervisees' performance in a manner that is clear and respectful.

PERFORMANCE EVALUATION

According to section 3.03 of the *Code of Ethics of the NASW (2018),* social workers that have responsibility for evaluating the performance of others should fulfill such responsibility in a fair and considerate manner and on the basis of clearly stated criteria.

CLIENT RECORDS

According to section 3.04 of the *Code of Ethics of the NASW (2018):*

- Social workers should take reasonable steps to ensure that documentation in records is accurate and reflects the services provided.
- Social workers should include sufficient and timely documentation in records to facilitate the delivery of services and to ensure continuity of services provided to clients in the future.
- Social workers' documentation should protect clients' privacy to the extent that is possible and appropriate and should include only information that is directly relevant to the delivery of services.
- Social workers should store records following the termination of service to ensure reasonable future access. Records should be maintained for the number of years required by state statutes or relevant contracts.

BILLING

According to section 3.05 of the *Code of Ethics of the NASW (2018),* social workers should establish and maintain billing practices that accurately reflect the nature and extent of services provided, and specifically by whom the service was provided in the practice setting.

RESOURCE ALLOCATION

According to section 3.07 of the *Code of Ethics of the NASW (2018),* social workers should advocate for resource allocation procedures that are open and fair. When not all clients' needs can be met, an allocation procedure should be developed that is nondiscriminatory and based on appropriate and consistently applied principles.

CONTINUING EDUCATION AND STAFF DEVELOPMENT

According to section 3.08 of the *Code of Ethics of the NASW (2018)*, social work administrators and supervisors should take reasonable steps to provide or arrange for continuing education and staff development for all staff for whom they are responsible. Continuing education and staff development should address current knowledge and emerging developments related to social work practice and ethics.

LABOR-MANAGEMENT DISPUTES

According to section 3.10 of the *Code of Ethics of the NASW (2018)*:

- Social workers may engage in organized action, including the formation of and participation in labor unions to improve services to clients and working conditions.
- The actions of social workers that are involved in labor-management disputes, job actions, or labor strikes should be guided by the professions' values, ethical principles, and ethical standards. Reasonable differences of opinion exist among social workers concerning their primary obligation as professionals during an actual or threatened labor strike or job action. Social workers should carefully examine relevant issues and their possible impact on clients before deciding on a course of action.

COMPETENCE

According to section 4.01 of the *Code of Ethics of the NASW (2018)*:

- Social workers should accept responsibility or employment only on the basis of existing competence or the intention to acquire the necessary competence.
- Social workers should strive to become and remain proficient in professional practice and the performance of professional functions.
- Social workers should critically examine, and keep current with, emerging knowledge relevant to social work. Social workers should routinely review professional literature and participate in continuing education relevant to social work practice and social work ethics.
- Social workers should base practice on recognized knowledge, including empirically based knowledge, relevant to social work and social work ethics.

DISCRIMINATION

According to section 4.02 of the *Code of Ethics of the NASW (2018)*, social workers should not practice, condone, facilitate, or collaborate with any form of discrimination on the basis of race, ethnicity, national origin, color, age, religion, sex, sexual orientation, marital status, political belief, or mental or physical disability.

PRIVATE CONDUCT

According to section 4.03 of the *Code of Ethics of the NASW (2018)*, social workers should not permit their private conduct to *interfere* with their ability to fulfill their professional responsibilities.

DISHONESTY, FRAUD, AND DECEPTION

According to section 4.04 of the *Code of Ethics of the NASW (2018)*, social workers should not participate in, condone, or be associated with *dishonesty, fraud, or deception.*

IMPAIRMENT

According to section 4.05 of the *Code of Ethics of the NASW (2018)*:

- Social workers should not allow their own personal problems, psychosocial distress, legal problems, substance abuse, or mental health difficulties to interfere with their professional judgment and performance or to jeopardize the best interests of people for whom they have a professional responsibility.
- Social workers whose personal problems, psychosocial distress, legal problems, substance abuse, or mental health difficulties interfere with their professional judgment and performance should immediately seek consultation and take appropriate remedial action by seeking professional help, making adjustments in workload, terminating practice, or taking any other steps necessary to protect clients and others.

MISREPRESENTATION

According to section 4.06 of the *Code of Ethics of the NASW (2018)*:

- Social workers should make clear distinctions between statements made and actions engaged in as a private individual and as a representative of the social work profession, a professional social work organization, or of the social worker's employing agency.
- Social workers who speak on behalf of professional social work organizations should accurately represent the official and authorized positions of the organization.
- Social workers should ensure that their representations to clients, agencies, and the public of professional qualifications, credentials, education, competence, affiliations, services provided, or results to be achieved are accurate. Social workers should claim only those relevant professional credentials they actually possess and take steps to correct any inaccuracies or misrepresentations of their credentials by others.

SOLICITATIONS

According to section 4.07 of the *Code of Ethics of the NASW (2018)*:

- Social workers should not engage in uninvited solicitation of potential clients who, because of their circumstances, are vulnerable to undue influence, manipulation, or coercion.
- Social workers should not engage in solicitation of testimonial endorsements (including solicitation of consent to use a client's prior statement as a testimonial endorsement) from current clients or other persons who, because of their particular circumstances are vulnerable to undue influence.

ACKNOWLEDGING CREDIT

According to section 4.08 of the *Code of Ethics of the NASW (2018)*:

- Social workers should take responsibility and credit, including authorship credit, only for work they have actually performed and to which they have contributed.
- Social workers should honestly acknowledge the work of and the contributions made by others.

EVALUATION AND RESEARCH

According to section 5.02 of the *Code of Ethics of the NASW (2018)*:

- Social workers should monitor and evaluate policies, the implementation of programs, and practice interventions.
- Social workers should promote and facilitate evaluation and research to contribute to the development of knowledge.
- Social workers should critically examine and keep current with emerging knowledge relevant to social work and fully use evaluation and research evidence in their professional practice.
- Social workers engaged in evaluation or research should carefully consider possible consequences and should follow guidelines developed for the protection of evaluation and research participants. Appropriate institutional review boards should be consulted.

INFORMED CONSENT FOR RESEARCH

According to section 5.02 of the *Code of Ethics of the NASW (2018)*:

- Social workers engaged in evaluation or research should obtain voluntary and written informed consent from participants, when appropriate, without any implied or actual deprivation or penalty for refusal to participate; without undue inducement to participate; and with due regard for participants' well-being, privacy, and dignity. Informed consent should include information about the nature, extent, and duration of the participation requested and disclosure of the risks and benefits of participation in the research.
- When using electronic technology to facilitate evaluation or research, social workers should ensure that participants provide informed consent for the use of such technology. Social workers should assess whether participants are able to use the technology and, when appropriate, offer reasonable alternatives to participate in the evaluation or research.

PATIENT RIGHTS IN RESEARCH

According to section 5.02 of the *Code of Ethics of the NASW (2018)*:

- Social workers should inform participants of their right to withdraw from evaluation and research at any time without penalty.
- Social workers should take appropriate steps to ensure that participants in evaluation and research have access to appropriate supportive services.
- Social workers engaged in evaluation or research should protect participants from unwarranted physical or mental distress, harm, danger, or deprivation.

PATIENT RIGHTS IN RESEARCH

According to section 5.02 of the *Code of Ethics of the NASW (2018)*:

- Social workers engaged in the evaluation of services should discuss collected information only for professional purposes and only with people professionally concerned with this information.
- Social workers engaged in evaluation or research should ensure the anonymity or confidentiality of participants and of the data obtained from them. Social workers should inform participants of any limits of confidentiality, the measures that will be taken to ensure confidentiality, and when any records containing research data will be destroyed.

- Social workers who report evaluation and research results should protect participants' confidentiality by omitting identifying information unless proper consent has been obtained authorizing disclosure.

LIABILITY FOR SOCIAL WORKERS

Elements of liability for social workers are as follows:

- Clients can sue social workers for malpractice.
- The chain of liability extends from the individual worker to supervisory personnel to the director and then to the board of directors of a nonprofit agency.
- Most agencies carry malpractice insurance, which usually protects individual workers, however, workers may also carry personal liability and malpractice insurance.
- Supervisors can be named as parties in a malpractice suit as they share vicarious liability for the activities of their supervisees.

IMPLICATIONS FOR CONFIDENTIALITY IF SOCIAL WORKER IS SUED FOR MALPRACTICE

A worker who is sued for malpractice may reveal information discussed by clients.

The worker should aim to limit the discussion of the content of clinical discussions to those statements needed to support an effective defense.

GENERAL RIGHTS FOR SOCIAL WORK CLIENTS

General rights for social worker clients include:

- Confidentiality and privacy.
- Informed consent.
- Access to services (if service requirements cannot be met, a referral should be offered).
- Access to records (adequately protective but not onerously burdensome policies for client access to services should be developed and put in place).
- Participation in the development of treatment plans (client cooperation in the treatment process is essential to success).
- Options for alternative services/referrals (clients should always be offered options whenever they are available).
- Right to refuse services (clients have a right to refuse services that are not court ordered; ethical issues exist when involuntary treatment is provided, but mandates do not allow options other than referrals to other sources of the mandated service).
- Termination by the client (clients have a right to terminate services at any time and for any reason they deem adequate, except in certain court-ordered situations).

RIGHT TO PRIVACY

Every individual has a right to expect that personal information disclosed in a clinical setting, including data such as their address, telephone number, Social Security number, financial information, and health information will not be disclosed to others, and no preconditions need be fulfilled to claim this right. The 1974 Federal Privacy Act (PL 93-579) also stipulates that clients be informed of the following:

- When records about them are being maintained.
- That they can access, correct, and copy these records.
- That the records are to be used only for the purpose of obtaining absent written consent otherwise.

Exceptions are:

- Need-to-know sharing with other agency employees.
- Use for research if identifying information is omitted.
- Release to the government for law enforcement purposes.
- Responding to a subpoena.
- In emergencies, where the health and safety of an individual is at risk. While the law applies only to agencies receiving federal funds, many state and local entities have adopted these standards.

HIPAA AND NASW ON CONFIDENTIALITY

In 1996 the federal government passed legislation providing privacy protection for personal health information. Known as **HIPAA** (Health Insurance Portability and Accountability Act), this act:

- Places privacy protections on personal health information and specifically limits the purposes for its use and the circumstances for its disclosure.
- Provides individuals with specific rights to access their records.
- Ensures that individuals will be notified about privacy practices. The act applies only to "covered entities," which are defined as health care providers (physicians and allied health care providers), clearinghouses for health care services, and health plans.

The National Association of Social Workers (**NASW**) has issued a policy on confidentiality. It provides general guidelines, including a client's right to be told of records being maintained and verification of the records for accuracy. It does not, however, specify how individuals may access these records.

UTILIZATION OF INFORMED CONSENT

A client may provide **consent** for the worker to share information with family members, or with other professionals or agencies for purposes of referral. When the client provides this consent, s/he has reason to expect that shared information is in her/his **best interest**, and designed to improve her/his situation. Through **informed consent**, a client may provide consent for the worker to share information with family members, or with other professionals or agencies for purposes of referral. When the client provides this consent, he or she has reason to expect that shared information is in his or her best interest, and designed to improve his or her situation.

CONFIDENTIALITY FOR SOCIAL WORKERS VS. LAWYERS OR CLERGY

Social work privilege does not have the same force as that of attorneys and clergy. Unlike clergy and attorneys, social workers may be compelled to testify in court under certain circumstances.

POLICIES REFLECTING EXPECTATION OF CONFIDENTIALITY

Organizational policies can reflect the expectation of confidentiality by:

- Records must be secured and locked.
- Policies should be in place that ensure that records not be left where unauthorized persons are able to read them.
- Computerized records should be secured with the same attention given to written records (hard copies).
- Agencies must provide spaces that permit private conversations so that conversations about clients can be held where they cannot be overheard.

Mandatory Reporting

REPORT THAT A CLIENT IS A DANGER TO SELF OR OTHERS

Reporting when a client is a danger to the self or others is mandated when:

- The client's *mental state* is such that s/he may deliberately or accidentally cause harm to self.
- The client makes a direct *threat* to harm another person and there is a reasonable possibility that s/he can carry out the threat.
- *Duty to warn*: All mental health professionals have a duty to warn individuals who are threatened. This principle was established by the Tarasoff Decision (*Tarasoff vs. Regents of University of California, 1976*).

IMPLICATIONS OF STATE MANDATES TO REPORT CHILD ABUSE

Every state in the U.S. has laws that mandate that social workers **report** the mere suspicion of child abuse to the appropriate authorities. A good faith report gives the worker **immunity** from civil or criminal liability if the report is not verified as social workers cannot be found liable for following the law. Informing clients of the worker's decision to make a report is determined situationally, particularly if there is a concern of the client's violent reaction to self or others.

CONCERNS WHEN REPORTING INCIDENTS OR SUSPICIONS OF SEXUAL ABUSE

The following are concerns when reporting incidents or suspicious sexual abuse:

- Perpetrators of these crimes can be highly motivated to obtain retractions and may threaten or use violence to do so.
- A major concern in developing immediate and long-term strategies for protection and treatment is the role of the non-abusing parent and his or her ability to protect the child.
- The victim may be safer if the worker does not notify the family when making the report.
- Great care must be taken by the worker with these cases.

ABUSE EVALUATION

Social workers are mandated reporters and must report all suspected cases of child abuse, in addition to "dependent adult" and elder abuse. When **assessing for signs of physical abuse**, note particularly the following:

- bruises, burns, cuts, or welts, and note if they are in various stages of healing
- attempts by the victim to hide injuries
- exaggerated efforts to please parents/caregivers
- major behavioral problems or disturbances (violence, withdrawal, self-injury, etc.)
- hypervigilance around adults, especially parents/caregivers.

Signs of psychological or emotional abuse include the following:

- Depression
- Withdrawal
- preoccupation with details
- repetitive, agitated, and/or rhythmic movements
- evidence of unreasonable demands or conflict triangulation (e.g., drawing a child into marital conflicts)

Signs of neglect include the following:

- inappropriate dress
- poor hygiene
- failure-to-thrive symptoms (delayed development, underweight, hair loss, begging for food, etc.)
- poor supervision
- significant fatigue
- missed school and/or medical appointments
- untreated health problems
- inadequate sleeping situation

FOLLOW UP AFTER IDENTIFYING CHILD, DEPENDENT ADULT, OR ELDER ADULT ABUSE

After abuse has been determined, a full report must be made to the appropriate agency, initially by telephone with a written report to follow. For social workers employed by such agencies, a follow-up plan of action must be determined. The level of risk must be evaluated, including the perpetrator's relationship to the victim, prior history of abusive behavior, and severity of harm inflicted, as well as the victim's age, health situation, cognitive capacity and psychological status, available support systems, and capacity for self-protection given that the abuse is now in the open.

Follow-up options include:

- Reports for criminal prosecution
- Home visits
- Removal from the home
- Alternative caregiver/guardian appointments through courts, etc.

Safety is the primary concern and is above all else.

Professional Development and Use of Self

PROFESSIONAL OBJECTIVITY IN SOCIAL WORKER-CLIENT RELATIONSHIP

Objectivity requires remaining neutral when making judgements. Because of the nature of social work, much evaluation tends to be subjective and not easily quantified, but these evaluations can then reflect the social worker and the social worker's biases. The goal should be to make objective observations as much as possible—reporting what is seen and heard rather than the opinion about those things. In order to ensure that opinions are objective, specific parameters should be developed for decision making. For example, if evaluating a client's socioeconomic status, judging by language and appearance may produce one opinion while judging according to occupation and income may produce another (and probably more accurate) opinion. The way a social worker measures may also reflect biases. For example, measuring gender by male and female only suggests a subjective rejection of other choices, such as binary or transgender.

PERFORMANCE APPRAISAL OF PROFESSIONAL SOCIAL WORKERS

Performance appraisals may vary from self-assessment, to narrative assessment, to check lists, and assessments based on outcomes related to a list of goals. Despite the varied forms of appraisal, basic skills are almost always evaluated:

- *Work-associated skills*: The ability to carry out the processes and procedures of social work, including applying appropriate interventions and dealing effectively with client problems and concerns.
- *Organizational skills*: The ability to manage time effectively and carry out job responsibilities in a timely and efficient manner.
- *Leadership/Management skills:* The ability to serve as a model for others, to influence other professionals, and to lead and supervise effectively.
- *Cultural competence*: An awareness of different cultures (including customs and religions) and understanding of cultural sensitivity when dealing with others.
- *Communication skills:* The ability to document and code correctly and to communicate effectively with co-workers and clients. Ability to use conflict resolution strategies and to accommodate various points of view.

SELF-CARE PRINCIPLES TO PREVENT OR ALLEVIATE BURNOUT AND SECONDARY TRAUMA

Burnout, a response to ongoing stress, is a problem pervasive in social work. Social workers often have excessive workloads and work long hours, often including unwanted overtime because of inadequate staffing. Social workers may feel that they have little control over their work and do not receive sufficient reward or support and that social workers are often treated unfairly or are victims of bullying in the workplace. Stress tends to build up over time, interfering with the individual's ability to concentrate and to carry out duties effectively. Additionally, dealing with clients' trauma may lead to **secondary trauma** with signs similar to PTSD--nightmares, insomnia, anxiety—increasing risk of burnout. Stages include:

1. Fight or flight response: Withdrawal, discord.
2. Emotional reaction: Anger, shock, surprise.
3. Negative thinking: Despair, anger, depression, anxiety.
4. Physical reaction: Headaches, GI upset, backache
5. No change in stressor or person: Increased stress.
6. Burnout.

Social workers may need to negotiate a smaller workload, utilize time management strategies, take small periodic breaks, and participate in stress management programs.

COMPASSION FATIGUE

Compassion fatigue can occur when people overly identify with the pain and suffering of others and begin to exhibit signs of stress as a result. These people are often empathetic, tend to place the needs of others above their own, and are motivated by the need to help others. Indications include:

- Blaming others and complaining excessively.
- Isolating oneself from others and having trouble concentrating.
- Exhibiting compulsive activities (gambling, drinking)
- Having nightmares, sleeping poorly, and exhibiting a change in appetite.
- Exhibiting sadness and/or apathy.
- Denying any problems and having high expectations of self and others.
- Having trouble concentrating.

- Questioning spiritual beliefs, losing faith.
- Exhibiting stress disorders: tachycardia, headaches, insomnia, pain.

Social workers who exhibit compassion fatigue may need to take a break from work in order to recover some sense of self and may benefit from stress management programs, cognitive behavioral therapy, relaxation and visualization exercises, and physical exercise.

TIME MANAGEMENT APPROACHES

Approaches that the social worker can utilize for **time management** include:

- Planning ahead: Maintaining a master schedule that lists visits and meetings.
- Keeping diary/schedule up-to-date on a daily basis.
- Utilizing color coding: Using colored stickers to indicate different needs, such as red stickers for those things that require urgent attention.
- Scheduling a time to return calls: Making calls first thing in the day so that any alterations needed in the schedule can be made promptly.
- Utilizing time management and/or case management software.
- Making appropriate referrals.
- Preparing reports (such as those submitted to the court) in advance, avoiding last minute rush.
- Making to-do lists or action plans.
- Creating templates for frequently used forms/letters.
- Filing immediately and throwing out unnecessary paperwork.
- Utilizing GPS and mapping software to plan routes of visits.
- Prioritizing work.
- Avoiding all procrastination.

ASWB Practice Test

1. A social worker has been called to conduct a mental status exam (MSE) with an 86-year-old elderly man who is suspected of having early symptoms of dementia. At one point the social worker asks him to interpret the idiom, "People who live in glass houses shouldn't throw stones." He responds, "Someone living in a glass house has to be careful, because stones can break glass." This response represents an example of:

    a. formal operational thought.
    b. pre-operational thought.
    c. sensorimotor interpretation.
    d. concrete operational thought.

2. The human and development and behavior theorist most closely associated with Functionalism is:

    a. John B. Watson
    b. William James
    c. Alfred Adler
    d. Lev Vygotsky

3. The theorist in human development and behavior who is most focused on moral development is:

    a. Lawrence Kohlberg.
    b. Margaret Mahler.
    c. Carol Gilligan.
    d. John Bowlby.

4. A key difference between the theorists Wilhelm Wundt and William James regarding cognitive and emotional responses to experiences is:

    a. James felt cognitive processing precedes emotions, while Wundt felt that emotions emerge prior to cognitive understanding.
    b. James felt emotional reactions precede cognitive processing, while Wundt felt that cognitive processing precedes emotional reactions.
    c. James felt that cognitive processing and emotions occur simultaneously, while Wundt felt emotions emerge before cognitive processing.
    d. James felt that cognitive processing precedes emotions, while Wundt felt that cognitive processing and emotions occur simultaneously.

5. Sigmund Freud proposed the concepts of *preconscious* and *unconscious* to describe thoughts, feelings and ideas that are outside of conscious awareness but that nevertheless influence behavior and thinking. The primary difference between preconscious and unconscious thought is:

    a. unconscious thoughts can never be brought to conscious awareness, while preconscious thoughts can only be brought to awareness with great difficulty.

    b. preconscious thoughts can never be brought to conscious awareness, while unconscious thoughts can be brought to awareness only with great difficulty.

    c. unconscious thoughts can be brought to awareness relatively easily, while preconscious thoughts are much more difficult to bring to awareness.

    d. preconscious thoughts can be brought to awareness relatively easily, while unconscious thoughts are much more difficult to bring to awareness.

6. An 11-year-old boy is seen in clinic for multiple episodes of stealing behavior, exclusively involving the theft of inexpensive toys from a local store. From the perspective of Freud's structure of personality, describe the driving personality force in this behavior and the MOST immediately effective intervention.

    a. The driving force is the Superego, and the most effective intervention would be an appeal to the child's sense of empathy for the needs of the store's owner

    b. The driving force is the Ego, and the most effective intervention would be to discuss acceptable ways to meet the desire for toys

    c. The driving force is the Id, and the most effective intervention would be to cite the negative consequences of the behavior

    d. The driving force is the Life Instinct, and the most effective intervention would be to examine the role of altruism in proper behavior

7. A 46-year-old woman is referred for treatment for nicotine and alcohol addiction. She is also some 150 pounds overweight. The client claims to "like smoking" with no desire to quit, denies the extent of her alcoholism, and suggests that she doesn't "really eat very much." From a Freudian perspective, the client may have a fixation in which of the following stages of Freud's five stages of psychosexual development?

    a. Latency Period

    b. Phallic Stage

    c. Anal Stage

    d. Oral Stage

8. A couple comes to see a social worker. Married just two years, they're having difficulty adjusting. He's the youngest in his family and she's the oldest, which seems at the root of some of their problems. For example, she feels he's being irresponsible, and he feels she's being harsh and uncaring of his situation. Specifically, he has been out of work for several months, and she's working a marginal, late-night waitressing job just to make ends meet. She's tired and upset, and wants him to take any of a number of jobs he has passed up. He's pushing for something even better than any in his past. To make matters worse, he's been making troubling purchases "just for fun," which have caused more financial burden. From an Adlerian perspective, which of the following would BEST explain their situation?

    a. Needs hierarchy and separation-individuation

    b. Ego vs Superego conflicts

    c. Birth order and guiding fiction

    d. Inferiority vs superiority

9. An 8-year-old girl is brought in by referral from a school counselor. The referral indicates the child is inordinately afraid of being outdoors, refusing recess periods and other normal play experiences. Accompanied by her mother, she seems quite shy and reserved. During the child's intake interview, the mother repeatedly interrupts questions about the child's various fears. Comments such as, "Well, of course she won't want to be on the playground! It's a dangerous place!" frequently emerge, along with voiced concerns about physical activity ("she could fall"), being outside on the sidewalk with friends ("a car could come by and hit them"), etc. Noting the mother's marked overprotective posture, the social worker draws upon which of the following theorists in considering a possible etiology of the problem?

    a. B. F. Skinner
    b. Ivan Pavlov
    c. Jean Piaget
    d. John B. Watson

10. A man comes in to see a social worker about a compulsion that is troubling him. Whenever someone brings up something very serious (a family death, grave illness, loss of a crucial job, or other major misfortune) he finds himself compelled to resort to humor to minimize the intense feelings involved. This has offended many people. During exploration of the problem, it is learned that his father was violently intolerant of any expression or display of negative emotion. Drawing upon Pavlovian theory, the client's compulsion can best be described as a/an:

    a. unconditioned stimulus.
    b. unconditioned response.
    c. conditioned stimulus.
    d. conditioned response.

11. When evaluating a 16-year-old girl's depression a social worker discovers that she's distressed, in part, because she has never learned to drive. Consequently, she's passed up occasional babysitting jobs, social events, and other activities. She feels inferior to others. Pointing this out to the parents, her father states, "She just can't learn. I've taken her driving and shown her what to do many times, but she isn't able to cut it." The social worker recommends enrollment in a professional driving class, but the father resists, saying, "There's nothing some driving instructor knows that I can't teach her." To overcome his resistance the social worker notes the unique driving tools available to an instructor and explain the concept of:

    a. behavior modification.
    b. interactive scaffolding.
    c. defense mechanisms.
    d. anaclitic depression.

12. An older woman who has recently lost her husband and been placed in a long-term nursing care facility because of impaired mobility is oppositional and refuses to participate in activities or eat scheduled meals, complaining that the staff members are "incompetent and rude" and that no one cares about what she wants. The woman is increasingly demanding to the point that staff members are avoiding her. Which action is most appropriate for the social worker to do FIRST?

    a. Counsel the staff members on methods of dealing with the woman
    b. Listen actively to the woman's complaints
    c. Advise the woman that her behavior is inappropriate
    d. Help the patient to devise a personal schedule of activities

13. A hospital social worker is assigned to work with families in an intensive care unit. A husband was recently told that his wife is terminally ill. In speaking with him, the social worker attempt to discuss his feelings about the impending loss of his wife and how he and his family are coping. However, the social worker finds the conversation persistently returning to recent medical tests, current physical indicators, and potential changes in her medications. This is an example of which of the following defense mechanisms?

    a. Projection
    b. Compensation
    c. Intellectualization
    d. Rationalization

14. A 32-year-old single woman comes to see a social worker about depression. The worker notices that she wears an excessive amount of makeup, dresses in teen-style attire, wears her hair in a faddish fashion, and uses a mixture of old and new era teen terms and language. As they talk, she narrates activities dominated by associations at teen and young adult clubs and haunts, and describes attempted relationships with individuals much younger than herself. When the social worker asks about peer relationships, she indicates that she avoids those her age as she does not want to become "old before her time," and sees herself as much more youthful that others her age. The defense mechanism she employs is BEST described as:

    a. avoidance.
    b. fixation.
    c. devaluation.
    d. affiliation.

15. A social worker is counseling a man at a walk-in community clinic. He had moved in with his girlfriend, but was recently evicted from her home. His way to work was by riding with her, and he now is unsure how to keep his job given the loss of transportation. This has left him with no stable living situation and in danger of unemployment. He has no family or close friends in the area. Emotionally, however, he is preoccupied with the loss of his relationship and the security and affection he found through it, which is all he wants to talk about. According to the theorist Abraham Maslow, the BEST response to this situation is to:

    a. go where the client wants to be, and work on his feelings about the relationship loss.
    b. refuse to talk about relationship issues until immediate needs regarding housing, transportation, and employment are met.
    c. permit some discussion on feelings of loss, but keep the focus on his immediate housing, transportation, and employment needs.
    d. explain to him that his needs are beyond what can be offered and refer him to a shelter program.

16. A 38-year-old man is being seen in an STI (sexually transmitted infections) clinic for treatment of chlamydia. The social worker has been called to discuss his sexual history with a focus on safe-sex practices, particularly while being treated. The social worker learns that he has a history of short-term sexual relationships with women, with many involving "one-night" encounters. He also admits to occasionally paying for sexual favors. According to the ego psychology theorist Erik Erikson, this client is struggling with mastery of which of the following stages of personality development?

    a. Stage 1: Trust vs. Mistrust
    b. Stage 5: Identity vs. Identify Diffusion
    c. Stage 6: Intimacy vs. Isolation
    d. Stage 8: Integrity vs. Despair

17. A 28-year-old woman comes to see you with complaints about rejection by her new boyfriend. They've been dating for about 6 weeks, and she notes that he's just no longer being as attentive as he was. She wants to know what to do to "win him back." Upon further inquiry the social worker learn that she's experienced this in all her prior dating relationships. The social worker further learn that she calls, texts, drops by, and otherwise attempts to stay in contact throughout every day. She voices great fear that he will soon leave her "like the others." As she talks, high lability is noted in her emotions, ranging from fear and anxiety to intense anger. She also uses frequent criticism of herself, suggesting she is "not worth" having a relationship with, etc. The social worker quickly recognizes symptoms of likely borderline personality disorder. In considering a treatment approach, the social worker draws upon Margaret Mahler's work, which posits that this disorder likely occurs from problematic experiences during:

    a. normal autism phase.
    b. symbiosis phase.
    c. differentiation (hatching) phase.
    d. rapprochement phase.

18. A normally well-behaved 15-year-old girl is being seen for her recent onset of conflict and behavior problems. The parents are overwhelmed and in need of direction. They have used a variety of behavioral modification techniques (e.g., lectures, restrictions, grounding, loss of privileges) without success. The behavior has become so problematic that it has impeded the father's normal overseas travel for work. With further inquiry, the social worker learns that the father's employment has taken him away for extensive periods in the child's life, but that she now has his nearly undivided attention. Drawing upon the operant conditioning work of B.F. Skinner, the social worker identifies the problem as one of:

    a. positive reinforcement.
    b. negative reinforcement.
    c. punishment.
    d. extinction.

19. The difference between Ivan Pavlov's conditioning and B.F. Skinner's operant conditioning is:

    a. Pavlovian conditioning deals with the modification of voluntary behavior via consequences, while Skinner's operant conditioning produces behavior under new antecedent conditions.
    b. Skinner's operant conditioning deals with the modification of voluntary behavior via consequences, while Pavlovian conditioning produces behavior under new antecedent conditions.
    c. Pavlovian conditioning deals exclusively with involuntary bodily functions, while Skinner's operant conditioning deals solely with voluntary behaviors.
    d. Skinner's operant conditioning deals exclusively with involuntary bodily functions, while Pavlovian conditioning deals solely with voluntary behaviors.

20. A couple is receiving counseling to overcome identified obstacles and increase marital satisfaction. In the course of several visits, the social worker becomes aware that the husband often speaks of his "duty" to his family and his obligation to "do right by them." Using Lawrence Kohlberg's multistage model of moral development, the social worker identifies the husband's level to be:

    a. Level 1: Stage 2.
    b. Level 2: Stage 4.
    c. Level 3: Stage 5.
    d. Level 3: Stage 6.

21. When the social worker is assessing a one-year-old's attachment to the child's mother, the mother and child are placed in a room with a one-way mirror so the interactions can be observed. The mother plays with the child for a few minutes and then leaves the room, and the child responds by crying, a typical reaction. When the mother then returns to the room, which FIRST action by the child suggests the child is securely attached to the mother?

    a. The child continues crying and resists contact with the mother
    b. The child hugs the mother and then calms
    c. The child acts ambivalently toward the mother
    d. The child clings to the mother and resists letting go

22. The social worker is working with a group of women who are substance abusers. The women come from a variety of ethnic and social groups and have little interaction. During sessions with the group, if the social worker is applying feminist theory, which of the following would the social worker stress?
 a. The differences among the women
 b. The individual functional abilities
 c. The women's position in patriarchal society
 d. The commonalities among the women

23. During what period of child development would evidence of childhood psychopathology most likely become apparent?
 a. Physical development
 b. Cognitive/intellectual development
 c. Sexual development
 d. Language development

24. Failure of an infant to crawl by which of the following ages would be cause for concern?
 a. 6 months
 b. 9 months
 c. 12 months
 d. None of the above

25. A 10-year-old girl is brought in by her parents for evaluation because she has unexpectedly experienced menarche. They are concerned about possible sexual abuse, though they acknowledge that no other symptoms are present. The FIRST and most appropriate social work response would be to:
 a. refer the child to a qualified pediatrician for examination.
 b. contact local child abuse authorities and make a suspected abuse referral.
 c. interview the child immediately for risks of sexual abuse.
 d. reassure the parents that this is not unexpected for the child's age.

26. The term *sandwich generation* refers to:
 a. the prevalence of fast-food consumption in the current era.
 b. the loss of whole family–present dinner time meals in the home.
 c. the pressure of couples still rearing children while being required to care for aging parents.
 d. the pressure between health problems of aging and rising retirement age requirements.

27. A school counselor is seeing an 8-year-old girl who has symptoms suggestive of reactive attachment disorder (aversion to accepting comfort and affection, even from familiar adults, particularly when distressed), which is strongly correlated with severe abuse and/or neglect. There is no evidence of sexual abuse, but ample evidence of excessive punishment, emotional abuse, and significant neglect. From social work training, the social worker is aware that the MOST likely perpetrator of such abuse of a child this age would be:
 a. the father.
 b. the mother.
 c. older siblings.
 d. another adult relative.

28. A home health referral indicates that an elderly client's caregiving needs are not fully met by the live-in caregiving son and daughter-in-law. The client is constantly left in a windowless back bedroom with no television or radio, and virtually never brought out. There are also signs of skin breakdown, isolation-induced depression, and questionable nourishment, all of which were addressed by the referring nurse. The caregivers now openly acknowledge they are not able (or willing) to meet the client's needs, so they openly support placement. However, they emphasize that they have given up employment to provide care, are living on the client's retirement funds, and note that the home (which could be sold to pay for care) has been left to them in a will. Consequently, they are unwilling to make the changes required for placement. The FIRST social work response should be to:

    a. accept that the caregiver's situation cannot be changed at this time.
    b. refer them to a caregiver education seminar coming up in 2 months.
    c. arrange a prompt extended family meeting to explore options.
    d. contact the local Adult Protective Services to report suspected abuse.

29. The social worker is conducting a home evaluation of a client with two children. One child is 8 years old and doing well in school, but the other child is 6 years old and has autism spectrum disorder. This child is non-verbal and cognitively impaired, and needs almost constant attention. The client admits to being overwhelmed at times and feeling like running away. Based on role theory, how would the social worker describe the client's situation?

    a. Role set
    b. Role strain
    c. Role conflict
    d. Role exit

30. A husband finds his wife is drinking too much. She often apologizes and indicates she'd like to get help, though she refuses to call and make an appointment. Eventually he calls for her, and sets up an appointment with the social worker. In exploring her drinking, the social worker learns that he does most of the shopping for groceries, and for the alcoholic beverages brought into the home. He reveals that he purchases the alcohol to keep peace, and because he knows she would suffer with symptoms of delirium tremens if she was left without any access to alcohol. Worried for the children, he would at times call into work claiming to be sick when he knew she was having a particularly bad drinking binge. His behavior is BEST described as:

    a. addictive.
    b. codependent.
    c. manipulative.
    d. maladaptive.

31. A hospital social worker has been called to evaluate a patient who has been dealing with a diagnosis of terminal cancer. Recently he came to his physician and offered him a considerable sum of money to pursue an unorthodox, unproven treatment. The physician tried to explain the problems with such treatment, but the patient remained insistent, and even accused the physician of being unwilling to seek a cure in deference to continuing to bill his insurance for other fruitless procedures and treatments. Deeply disturbed, the physician referred the patient to the social worker. After speaking with the client and confirming the above, the social worker recognized the symptoms as characteristic of:

    a. a psychotic break.
    b. chemotherapy toxicity.
    c. grief bargaining.
    d. acute denial.

32. The social worker has two 10-year-old clients from similar traumatic and abusive backgrounds, but one client seems resilient and functions well, getting good grades in school and interacting well with friends, while the other client has become depressed and withdrawn, is failing most classes, and has no friends. Which of the following is the FIRST step to building resilience in the withdrawn 10-year-old?

    a. Providing positive reinforcement
    b. Providing opportunities for the child to be successful
    c. Facilitating an attachment to a nurturing adult
    d. Encouraging the child to try different strategies

33. The social worker wants to conduct research on social change and is considering a number of different theories as the basis for study. If the social worker is interested in how resources and power are distributed and determines that the conflict theory is the most appropriate, what is the FIRST question that the social worker would pose?

    a. Who is oppressed?
    b. What is the meaning?
    c. What is the function?
    d. Who most benefits?

34. A social worker is interviewing a client from a different culture. The client is encouraged to tell stories about his life from a cultural perspective, stories about traditions, history, and culture-specific experiences. Even though the client speaks English, a skilled interpreter is present to capture and elucidate unique idioms, phrases, and terms that have a unique meaning from within the client's cultural context. Listening carefully for underlying feelings and cultural meanings, the social worker restates important concepts, and incorporates the unique terms into the overall narrative. This form of engagement is referred to as:

    a. conceptual reframing.
    b. ethnographic paraphrasing.
    c. ethnographic interviewing.
    d. conceptual exploration.

35. The difference between the *nurturing system* and the *sustaining system* is:

   a. the nurturing system refers to family and intimate supports, while the sustaining system refers to institutional supports and society as a whole.

   b. the sustaining system refers to family and intimate supports, while the nurturing system refers to institutional supports and society as a whole.

   c. the nurturing system refers to educational opportunities and support, while the sustaining system refers to employment opportunities and support.

   d. the sustaining system refers to educational opportunities and support, while the nurturing system refers to employment opportunities and support.

36. Working at a bicultural community counseling center for Southeast Asian families, a social worker encounters a family troubled by sharp divisions between older family members and their young children. In particular, from the parent's viewpoint, the children seem to have lost respect for their elders, often treating their parents and even their grandparents in dismissive ways. According to Robbins, Chatterjee, and Canada (1998) this is evidence of:

   a. traditional adaptation.

   b. marginal adaptation.

   c. assimilation.

   d. bicultural adaptation.

37. A study attempts to measure the efficacy of a new antidepressant medication. A "control" group of depression sufferers will receive only a placebo, while an "intervention" group will receive the new medication. In this study, the "null hypothesis" would state the following:

   a. the intervention group will report fewer symptoms of depression than the control group.

   b. the control group will report fewer symptoms of depression than the intervention group.

   c. both the control group and the intervention group will report fewer numbers of depressive symptoms.

   d. there shall be no measurable difference in depression symptom reporting between the control group and the intervention group.

38. A 32-year-old client living with two adolescent children (13 and 15) in a temporary shelter for battered women and their children did not graduate from high school and has never held a job because her ex-partner believed women should stay in the home and care for children. The social worker has assisted the client to apply for welfare benefits. Which of the following is likely the best additional intervention to lift the client and her family from poverty?

   a. Assist the client in finding a job

   b. Encourage the client to return to school and attend college

   c. Advise the client to continue to depend on welfare benefits

   d. Enroll the client in a job training program

39. A social worker is working with a 22-year-old woman who is grappling with her emerging sexual identity as a lesbian. She expresses comfortable acceptance of her lesbianism, and indicates meaningful support from an extended circle of friends in the LGBT community. Even so, she has yet to reveal her sexuality to her heterosexual friends and family, citing fears of rejection and stating that she is embarrassed to take this very difficult step. According to Robins, Chatterjee, and Canada (1998), this client is in which of the following stages of the Coming Out Process?

   a. Stage 2: Identity recognition
   b. Stage 4: Disclosure
   c. Stage 7: Pride in identity
   d. Stage 8: Increased disclosure

40. In the LGBT community, the term *intersex* refers to:

   a. ambiguous sexual anatomy (hermaphrodite).
   b. heterosexual orientation.
   c. sexual encounters outside of preference.
   d. sexual attraction to both men and women.

41. A 46-year-old woman has come in with complaints of depression. Attempts at exploration of the underlying issues reveal numerous long-standing challenges (work, marriage, children), but no clear precipitating event(s). Along with dysphoria, the client has clear vegetative symptoms as well (anorexia, insomnia, fatigue, anhedonia, and impaired attention). Other than ventilation and support, what should be the social worker's FIRST response in this situation?

   a. Press the client further in seeking a precipitating depressive event
   b. Refer the client to a psychiatrist for antidepressant evaluation
   c. Begin working with the client's denial about depressive issues in her life
   d. Refer the client to a primary care physician for a health evaluation

42. A 72-year-old Caucasian man comes in to see the social worker with symptoms of depression. Although widowed, he has a supportive extended family, is well educated, generally financially solvent, and has only typical age-related health concerns (moderate arthritis, borderline high blood pressure, and a pacemaker). Successful throughout his life, he has a very stable history. During the conversation he makes a passing comment about "wondering if life is worth it anymore." The BEST response to this somewhat offhand comment would be to:

   a. ignore it as a common phrase that shouldn't be troubling.
   b. note it, but wait to see of similar feelings arise again.
   c. reassure him that life is always worth living, even if challenging.
   d. key in on the phrase and inquire directly about suicidal thoughts.

43. The social worker has a special interest in assisting clients who are attempting to move from welfare benefits to the world of work. Which of the following would best indicate that the social worker is activity promoting economic justice?

   a. Establishing partnerships with industry to train and employ clients
   b. Explaining to clients that they have the right to equal pay for equal work
   c. Serving on an economic justice committee with a professional organization
   d. Conducting in-service training for other social workers on economic justice

44. A social worker is seeing a recently returned 26-year-old male military veteran who had been deployed on active duty in the Middle East. He has obvious symptoms of posttraumatic stress disorder (PTSD) (intrusive memories, flashbacks, hypervigilance, angry outbursts, etc.). The social worker should explore the possibility of all of the following as potential causes of these symptoms EXCEPT:

 a. combat stress.
 b. disciplinary issues.
 c. mild traumatic brain injury (MTBI).
 d. sexual assault trauma.

45. The National Association of Social Workers (NASW) has established a clear position with regard to undocumented (illegal) immigrants. The position includes all of the following EXCEPT:

 a. advocating for rights and services for undocumented residents.
 b. transitioning undocumented immigrants back to their homeland.
 c. opposing any mandatory immigration reporting by social workers.
 d. facilitating documentation and benefits for undocumented residents.

46. During an intake interview, key areas of data collection include all of the following categories EXCEPT:

 a. problem areas, strengths, and support systems.
 b. attitude and motivation.
 c. insurance and ability to pay.
 d. relationships, resources, and safety.

47. The social worker has increasing numbers of clients who are refugees from third world countries, such as Somalia, and notes that many exhibit signs of depression (withdrawal, crying, insomnia, sadness) but are very resistant to any type of referral to mental health services, denying that they have a problem. What is the most likely reason for this response?

 a. Different attitude toward mental illness
 b. Lack of education
 c. Fear of medical interventions
 d. Resentment toward healthcare providers

48. In the clinical setting a social worker is asked to assess clients based upon their complaints, deficits, and identified problems. This method of assessment draws upon which of the following assessment models?

 a. Strengths perspective
 b. Medical model
 c. Biopsychosocial model
 d. None of the above

49. An adolescent client in foster care repeatedly complains of various ailments, but symptoms usually subside shortly after the client is allowed to stay home from school, suggesting the client is feigning illness. Which of the following is the most appropriate response?

    a. "It's clear that you are not really ill, so you need to explain why you are pretending."

    b. "You can't continue to pretend to be sick morning after morning because school is important."

    c. "I can see that you are avoiding school because of something that may be difficult for you to talk about."

    d. "Pretending to be sick is very dishonest, and you have to stop."

50. A client arrives for services at a community counseling clinic. He is pleasant, easily engaged, and discusses the need to work on "some interpersonal problems." When asked about any prior treatment, he notes that he has been seen by another social worker for the past 8 months. However, he now needs to seek services closer to home due to a change in his work schedule. When presented with an information release for contact with his prior social worker he becomes agitated and upset, and refuses to allow the contact. The BEST response in this situation would be to:

    a. accept the client's need to keep his therapeutic past private.

    b. discuss his concerns and support him, but require the collateral contacts.

    c. refuse services to the client based on his refusal to permit collateral contacts.

    d. do none of the above.

51. During a Friday afternoon counseling visit, a client voices thoughts about suicide. She does not appear to be emotionally overwrought, but rather seems peaceful and calm. She discusses that she feels she has accomplished all she can in life, particularly given the poor relationship she has with her husband and the fact that the last of their children recently left home. She notes having read some online information about a cardiac medication she takes (Digoxin), and believes that an overdose of this medication would precipitate rapid cardiac arrest. She just had the prescription refilled, and is just considering when to act—perhaps when her husband is out golfing the next Sunday morning. The FIRST appropriate response to this information should be to:

    a. call 911 to ensure the client receives immediate help for her suicidal intent.

    b. call local law enforcement to involuntarily escort the client for further suicide evaluation and hospitalization.

    c. complete a suicide risk evaluation, and then arrange voluntary hospitalization if the client will accept it.

    d. create a very detailed suicide prevention contract with the client, and plan several sessions to address her suicidality.

52. A social worker is seeing a married couple, at times individually. During an individual session the husband reveals that he is bisexual. He also reveals a lengthy history of sexual liaisons with other men and discloses that he recently learned he is HIV positive (via confirmatory tests through his primary care physician). Inquiring, the social worker discovers that he has not disclosed his HIV status to his spouse and that he does not use any barrier protection when with her. Upon explaining the life-and-death risk to his wife, he still maintains that he won't change this behavior. He first minimizes the risk, and then claims she would "suspect something" if he started using protection. After lengthy counseling he remains unwilling to either reveal his HIV status or to use protection. According to recent interpretations of the Tarasoff Case the social worker's duty now is to:

    a. contact the client's wife to inform her of the danger.
    b. contact the client's physician to inform him/her of the problem.
    c. report the case to the department of public health.
    d. continue this as a priority counseling topic.

53. A mental status exam (MSE) covers all the following domains EXCEPT:

    a. addictions and compulsions.
    b. appearance and attitude.
    c. mood and affect.
    d. insight and judgment.

54. An 8-year-old child has an out-of-home placement in a temporary foster home because of severe neglect and abandonment by her parents. The child had been found after living alone in a filthy apartment for a week. The child reports that she has one younger sibling but does not know the location of the child. What should be the FIRST consideration of the social worker?

    a. Locating the parents
    b. Locating kin
    c. Locating permanent foster parents
    d. Locating the sibling

55. While the use of the multiaxial system in *DSM-IV* has been removed from *DSM-5*, the use of specifiers continues. The purpose of diagnostic specifiers is to:

    a. offer clinical justification.
    b. delineate subtypes and severity.
    c. differentiate between related diagnoses.
    d. indicate uncertainty.

56. In determining the degree of severity of an intellectual disability, the most important determinant is:

    a. IQ score.
    b. adaptive functioning.
    c. intellectual functioning.
    d. deficits in person responsibility.

57. In working with an 11-year-old girl, it is noted that she seems to have limited verbal skills, including problems in word selection and use. Intelligence testing indicates normal cognitive capacity. Other testing has not shown any sensory impairments or other medical conditions. These early indicators are BEST suggestive of which of the following tentative diagnoses?

    a. Speech sound disorder
    b. Childhood-onset fluency disorder
    c. Autism spectrum disorder
    d. Language disorder

58. An 8-year-old boy presents with a number of complex developmental deficits. In particular, the child seems to isolate himself as evidenced by an apparent disinterest (or perhaps inability) in communicating with others, an idiosyncratic use of words and language, little imaginative play or social imitation, poor peer relationships, limited responses to others in his presence even if engaged, and odd, repetitive motions, routines, and rituals. The most likely tentative diagnosis would be:

    a. social (pragmatic) communication disorder.
    b. intellectual disability.
    c. autism spectrum disorder.
    d. language disorder.

59. A homeless client was a victim of an assault, resulting in a broken nose and multiple bruises, and is being treated in an emergency department. The social worker urges the client to file a complaint with the police because he is the fourth homeless person to be assaulted recently and recognized the perpetrator, but the client refuses to file a complaint because of distrust of the police. Which of the following is the best response?

    a. "If you receive medical care, you must report the incident to the police."
    b. "Let the doctor treat you and then you can decide later about filing a complaint."
    c. "I understand. You don't have to report the incident."
    d. "If you don't file a complaint, more people will be assaulted."

60. A social worker in a medical clinic is called to evaluate a 15-year-old girl who admits to persistent eating of paper products. The problem has persisted for some 6 months, and has led to minor weight loss and some level of poor nutrition. The preferred paper for ingestion is tissue paper, either toilet roll paper or facial tissues. The parents first noted the problem when tissue products continually disappeared in the home. There has also been some evidence of her ingesting other nonfood materials, such as clay, and sand, and obvious evidence of her consuming an inordinate amount of ice chips. The parents report that the patient is eating meals normally otherwise. The patient is reluctant to talk about any of this, just saying things such as "I don't know" and "maybe" and "I guess" to most any inquiry, and/or growing silent. The MOST LIKELY tentative diagnosis would be:

    a. pica.
    b. bulimia nervosa.
    c. anorexia nervosa.
    d. rumination disorder.

61. When used in reference to an individual who is chronologically at least 4 years old (or, mentally, at least 4 years old), the term *encopresis* refers to:

    a. the voluntary expelling of fecal matter in an inappropriate place.
    b. the involuntary expelling of fecal matter in an inappropriate place.
    c. the expelling of fecal matter in response to symptoms of stress or anxiety.
    d. all of the above.

62. A mother brings in her 8-year-old daughter due to her inability to sleep in her own bed at night. The mother has a history of sleeping with her daughter since about age 2, when she became divorced. She has, however, recently remarried and the daughter's insistence to sleep in the bed with her mother has become extremely problematic. When efforts are made to send the daughter to her own bed (in a room alone) the daughter becomes extremely stressed, tearful, and eventually displays tantrum-like behavior that fully disrupts sleep for the household until she is allowed to sleep with her mother. The MOST LIKELY diagnosis for this behavior would be:

    a. Oppositional-Defiant Disorder.
    b. Separation Anxiety Disorder.
    c. Agoraphobia.
    d. Panic Disorder.

63. Delirium differs from encephalopathy in which of the following ways?

    a. Delirium has a sudden onset, while encephalopathy is gradual
    b. Delirium involves sepsis, while encephalopathy involves toxins
    c. Delirium has a gradual onset, while encephalopathy is sudden
    d. None of the above

64. A social worker is called to evaluate a 78-year-old man (per his driver's license) found wandering by police, who was seen in the emergency department for "altered mental status." Staff suggest he appears "senile" and is probably in need of placement in a residential care setting. Upon meeting the patient, the social worker screens him using the Folstein Mini-Mental State Exam (MMSE). He is indeed confused, disoriented, forgetful, and otherwise cognitively impaired. Medical staff note he has no emergent condition. He is not febrile (no fever) or septic (only slightly elevated white blood cell count), no respiratory distress (breathes easily), and no cardiac compromise (age-expected elevated blood pressure and heart rate, with normal cardiac sounds and ECG tracing). No family can be reached; no information about prescription medication is available. The BEST social work response in this situation is to:

    a. record "probable dementia" and arrange out-of-home placement.
    b. arrange patient transportation back home with a home health referral.
    c. delay any response until family or other collateral contact can be made.
    d. advocate for the patient to be admitted for further medical evaluation.

65. The social worker is interviewing a 48-year-old male after receiving a referral from adult protective services. The man appears unkempt, and his apartment is dirty and garbage-filled. The man exhibits confusion, disorganized speech, and flat affect. The social worker notes a number of medication bottles on a nearby table and asks to review them: hydrochlorothiazide, clozapine, acetaminophen, simvastatin, and lisinopril. The social worker recognizes that clozapine is a psychotropic medication. What should the social worker's FIRST action be?

    a. Ask the man why he is taking clozapine
    b. Check the date on the clozapine and other medication bottles and the numbers of pills remaining
    c. Contact the physician listed on the medication bottle
    d. Recommend a 72-hour psychiatric hold

66. A chemical dependency counselor is counseling a 38-year-old married man regarding his ongoing use of alcohol. The client consumes alcohol on weekends and at parties, and tends to drink heavily about twice each month. At times, recovery from significant inebriation has resulted in his being unable to go to work on a Monday, and on one occasion he was given a DUI citation, resulting in this court-ordered counseling. The pattern of the client's alcohol use is best described as:

    a. alcohol intoxication.
    b. alcohol use disorder.
    c. recreational alcohol use.
    d. alcohol withdrawal.

67. In a county psychiatric emergency clinic, a social worker is asked to evaluate a 19-year-old woman for unspecified psychotic behavior. She is accompanied by her parents, who brought her to the clinic. Upon contact it is noted that she is disheveled and unkempt in grooming and hygiene. In talking with the social worker, she often pauses inexplicably, rambles about something unrelated, laughs to herself, and then turns her face away. Episodically attending to the social worker, she spontaneously claims that the worker is controlling her mind, and indicates that she sees odd objects floating around the social worker. There is no recent history of substance abuse (though remotely positive for amphetamines), and her symptoms have been prominent for most of the past year, though particularly acute this evening when she attacked her mother claiming that she was a clone and trying to pull her "real mom" out of the clone's body. The most likely diagnosis for this presentation is:

    a. bipolar disorder.
    b. schizoaffective disorder.
    c. schizophrenia.
    d. substance-induced psychosis.

68. A 34-year-old man makes an appointment to see a social worker for help coping with a difficult relationship in his life. At intake the social worker learns that he feels a famous movie actress has hidden affection for him. He has written her many times through her fan club, and has received letters from club personnel—never from the actress herself. But, he explains, this is just because she's "not currently free to express her feelings openly" due to a waning relationship with a wealthy businessman. When talking about the businessman, there are clear feelings of competition. When asked for greater detail or information to buttress his beliefs he avoids the questions. The MOST appropriate early diagnostic impression would be Delusional Disorder, with the following subtype:

    a. grandiose type.
    b. jealous type.
    c. persecutory type.
    d. erotomanic type.

69. A call is received from a family member about an adult male loved one who is "behaving in an extremely bizarre way." Specifically, he is racing from home to home, claiming that he is being followed by some sort of assault team (SWAT) intent on arresting him. He claims that people are hiding in cars all around him, even going so far as to claim entire parking lots are filled with cars hiding his assailants. He insists on pulling drapes and hiding out in the home for his safety. No evidence corroborates his story. He does have a history of deployment in Middle East combat, as well as a history of substance abuse, though neither presents as proximal to this event. By the next morning he appears fine, and becomes angry if the incident is brought up, suggesting it is all an exaggeration by others. The MOST appropriate diagnostic impression would be:

    a. posttraumatic stress disorder, acute episode.
    b. brief psychotic disorder.
    c. drug-induced psychosis.
    d. bipolar disorder, manic episode.

70. A social worker has been called to evaluate a 28-year-old female client described as "very depressed." Upon assessment the worker discovers that she has been struggling with depression since her late teens. She also admits to periods when she's entirely free of depression, even to the extent of thinking the problem is solved. Further questioning reveals that her depressions are quite deep, though not entirely anhedonic or debilitating, nor are her "up" periods marked by extremes in mood, grandiosity, insomnia, etc. Even so, her up and down phases are significant enough to disrupt relationships, work, and school (e.g., feeling unable to get out of bed when down, and pressured speech and euphoria to the extent to make others uncomfortable). Given this presentation, the MOST appropriate diagnostic impression would be:

    a. bipolar disorder.
    b. dysthymia.
    c. cyclothymia.
    d. mood disorder NOS.

71. A 72-year-old widow comes to see a social worker for help with feelings of bereavement. Her spouse died of a sudden heart attack just over a year ago. There was no prior history of a heart condition, so the loss came as a substantial shock and without forewarning. Since that time the client feels she has been unable to recover emotionally. She notes remaining intensely preoccupied with thinking about her husband, cries more days than not, feels estranged from others in many ways without him (e.g., other friends and couples seem distant), and describes her emotions as generally numb, when not overwhelming. Sometimes she yearns to die so that she can "be with him" again. There is no overt suicidality, but there is a feeling that life without him is meaningless in many ways. The MOST appropriate early diagnostic impression would be:

   a. major depressive disorder.
   b. posttraumatic stress.
   c. uncomplicated bereavement.
   d. persistent complex bereavement disorder.

72. The key difference between Bipolar I and Bipolar II is:

   a. Bipolar I involves mania and Bipolar II involves primarily depression.
   b. Bipolar I involves primarily depression and Bipolar II involves mania.
   c. Bipolar I involves hypomania and Bipolar II involves dysthymia.
   d. None of the above.

73. A social worker has been called to evaluate a 23-year-old man in a hospital emergency room. He presented with fear that he was having a heart attack, but medical staff have ruled this out following laboratory and clinical testing. He notes that his symptoms have subsided, but that when he arrived his heart was pounding, he was tremulous, gasping for breath, and had significant tightness in his chest. He recognized the symptoms as being cardiac in nature, as his father died recently from a heart attack when similar symptoms were present. After lengthy discussion he revealed that the symptoms had been coming and going rapidly over the last month, and that he had actually been sleeping in his car outside the hospital for the last several days to ensure he could get help when needed. The symptoms struck and peaked quickly (within minutes), leaving him fearful that help would not be available if he didn't remain close. These symptoms MOST closely resemble:

   a. anxiety disorder due to a medical condition.
   b. generalized anxiety disorder.
   c. acute stress disorder.
   d. panic disorder.

74. A social worker is called to a medical clinic to evaluate a 56-year-old woman who presents with persistent fears of a new diagnosis of melanoma. She had a small skin lesion removed from her nose approximately 2 years ago, which had precancerous tissue changes upon evaluation by pathology. Since that time, she has become intensely preoccupied with the status of her skin, and tends to check and recheck every blemish that occurs. Frequent visits to her dermatologist have not resulted in the identification of any new dermatological problems, and despite reassurances her worries continue unabated. The problem has grown to the point that she regularly asks her spouse to help her monitor her skin and examine her back to ensure no new problems. He has grown increasingly frustrated. She also refuses to go outdoors unless overly swathed to ward off any exposure to the sun. This has resulted in her increasingly avoiding the outdoors altogether. The MOST likely diagnosis for her presentation is:

    a. Malingering Disorder.
    b. Factitious Disorder.
    c. Illness Anxiety Disorder.
    d. Somatic Symptom Disorder.

75. A client is brought into a county mental health clinic by law enforcement. He has no personal identification, and cannot recall any personally identifying information. This forgetfulness appears to be genuine, not due to any threat or allegation of any kind. He does have receipts and other papers on his person that indicate he was recently many hundreds of miles away, but he cannot confirm or deny this. There is no history of head trauma, substance abuse, or prior mental illness that can be ascertained. The MOST appropriate initial working diagnosis would be:

    a. dissociative identity disorder.
    b. dissociative amnesia with dissociative fugue.
    c. depersonalization/derealization disorder.
    d. dissociative trance.

76. A newly married 23-year-old woman has been referred for counseling due to her experiences of painful intercourse. She was not sexually active prior to marriage, and so there is no history to draw upon for past experiences. The problem is painful penetration, not involving spasms of the vagina but characterized by marked vaginal dryness. The proper term for her condition is:

    a. female sexual interest/arousal disorder.
    b. genito-pelvic pain disorder.
    c. substance/medication induced sexual dysfunction.
    d. female orgasmic disorder.

77. A 26-year-old woman is seeing a social worker regarding her persistent desire to leave her bedroom window blinds open so that she might be seen disrobing by her male neighbor, who participates voyeuristically in an open way. She is aware that the activity is fraught with problems—he is a married man, and potentially other passersby might see in her window from the street. To this point, however, she finds these risks somewhat exciting and stimulating. She also finds herself compulsively thinking about the activity and planning ways to be "caught" by the man in compromising moments. Diagnostically, her behavior is best described as:

    a. frotteurism.
    b. voyeurism.
    c. exhibitionism.
    d. other specified paraphilia.

78. During an interview with a 15-year-old client, the client persists in making suggestive remarks about the social worker's appearance and asks if the social worker is married or has a partner. Which of the following is the most appropriate response?

    a. "Stop making those comments and asking questions."
    b. "It's not appropriate for us to discuss personal information, and I feel uncomfortable with your comments."
    c. "Why are you talking like this?"
    d. "If you continue making these types of comments, you will need to work with another social worker."

79. A social worker has been seeing a 26-year-old female client for about 6 months. She originally came to see the social worker about distress over a recent romantic relationship breakup. Over time the worker has learned that she tends to have serial relationships of short duration, which inevitably end badly. A common theme in the relationships is a pattern of over-idealizing, rejecting, and then clinging and trying to avoid perceived abandonment. Her mood is often labile, and she frequently follows a similar pattern in the counseling relationship: praising the social worker effusively and then later accusing him of neglect, professional incompetence, and bias, etc. The social worker has learned that she had poor childhood attachment with her parents, with a substantial history of physical abuse by them both. It now appears that the early primary diagnosis of adjustment disorder would now be coupled with:

    a. Histrionic Personality Disorder.
    b. Narcissistic Personality Disorder.
    c. Borderline Personality Disorder.
    d. Antisocial Personality Disorder.

80. Face-to-face work with clients is often described as:

    a. direct practice.
    b. clinical practice.
    c. micro practice.
    d. all of the above.

81. The social worker is utilizing role playing in group therapy with a client who has problems with interpersonal relationships and anger management. The first technique involved identifying a problem and the client enacting his role in the situation with a partner. The social worker then suggests they practice mirroring. What would this involve?
   a. The partner reflects the behavior displayed by the client
   b. The client enacts the role of the partner
   c. The client acts out an imaginary future interaction
   d. The client reenacts the role in an idealized manner

82. A crisis is an event that threatens or upends a state of equilibrium in ways that breach the coping capacity of the participants involved—usually a threat or obstacle to important relationships or goals. All of the following are major types of crises that may need to be addressed EXCEPT:
   a. cultural/societal.
   b. transitional.
   c. maturational.
   d. situational.

83. The social worker's client is a single mother with few resources and many issues: three young children, unemployed, homeless, victim of intimate partner abuse, and a long history of alcohol abuse. The client and her children are currently living in a temporary shelter. If utilizing the principle of partialization, which of the following would the social worker do FIRST?
   a. Make a list of resources
   b. Ask the client what she wants to deal with first
   c. Choose one-half of problems to focus on
   d. Make a list of problems

84. The *Premack Principle* refers to:
   a. a guideline for crisis intervention.
   b. a tool for managing intra-family conflicts.
   c. a process for improving client rapport.
   d. a method for increasing desired behaviors.

85. A contingency contract is used in behavior modification to:
   a. ensure a specific response for a specific behavior.
   b. provide a reward for specific behavior.
   c. provide a punishment for a specific behavior.
   d. all of the above.

86. There is strong empirical evidence that the therapeutic approach and treatment of choice for depression should be:
   a. cognitive-behavioral therapy.
   b. reality therapy.
   c. behavior modification.
   d. Critical Incident Stress Management.

87. A client comes to see a social worker, citing problems with choosing a career. Working collaboratively the social worker assists in clarifying the problem and identifying outcome goals, with specific steps to engage and achieve the goals and concluded by feedback and evaluation of client progress. From this process it is clear that the model of intervention being used is BEST described as:

    a. dialectical behavioral therapy.
    b. reality therapy.
    c. solution-focused therapy.
    d. none of the above.

88. The Neo-Freudian psychotherapist that differed from Freud's views primarily on the root origins of anxiety was:

    a. Erich Fromm.
    b. Karen Horney.
    c. Harry Stack Sullivan.
    d. None of the above.

89. A 32-year-old male veteran has come to see a social worker over troubling dreams that have persisted long after his return to the United States. The dreams involve reliving combat experiences in which he sees the deaths of important colleagues. Together, they work to relieve and psychologically reconcile these events, allowing the client to discharge the pent-up emotions associated with them. This psychotherapeutic approach is known as:

    a. reorientation.
    b. catharsis.
    c. purging.
    d. abreaction.

90. The term introjection is used differently between psychoanalysis and Gestalt therapy. Specifically, in Gestalt therapy the term refers to:

    a. failing to produce a boundary that defines a unique sense of self.
    b. modeling oneself after relationally important caregiving adults.
    c. living into the labels that others place on us.
    d. gradually defining oneself, by rejection or integration of outside ideas.

91. A social worker has been asked to facilitate an ongoing group experience for young married couples. The goals are relationship enrichment, with a particular focus on marital success after the birth of their children and in the press of career development. The group meets weekly, with no set termination date. This group is best described as:

    a. an open-ended socialization group.
    b. an ongoing support group.
    c. an open educational group.
    d. an ongoing growth group.

92. The social worker is working on a project with a coworker who persists in berating the social worker for missing a meeting scheduled when the social worker had to deal with a client emergency. The social worker needs to ask for information but realizes this will give the coworker another opportunity to complain. Which of the following exemplifies the most effective assertive communication?

    a. "Can you review the data with me so I can get up-to-date."
    b. "I'm so sorry that I missed the meeting, but can you review the data with me."
    c. "I realize I missed the meeting and that was inconvenient for you, but what did the data show?"
    d. "I'll try to review the data before we meet again."

93. In seeing a couple with significant conflict issues, a number of hot-point issues begin to emerge. In avoiding taking sides, the social worker is seeking to prevent:

    a. coaching.
    b. triangulation.
    c. identity fusion.
    d. emotional cutoff.

94. In Communications/Experimental Therapy, the idea that the same results can be secured in different ways is referred to as:

    a. circular causality.
    b. relational symmetry.
    c. equifinality.
    d. complementary conclusion.

95. A 4-year-old child has been placed into foster care because his father is unknown and his mother has been charged with child endangerment after leaving the child unattended while she engaged in prostitution. The child is otherwise healthy and appears to have been well cared for, but this is the second foster care placement for the child for the same reason. When engaging in permanency planning for the child, which of the following should be the FIRST goal?

    a. Family reunification with mother
    b. Kinship placement with family
    c. Long-term foster care
    d. Adoption by unrelated family

96. A couple in their 40s have come in to manage conflict issues in their marriage and family. In particular, neither can agree on basic roles as a couple. Both work outside the home; both tend to retain their income independently; each feels the other should be paying a greater portion of the bills; neither wants to be responsible for cooking, shopping, or housecleaning. According to Salvador Minuchin's Structural Family Theory, the couple is struggling with:

    a. complementarity.
    b. alignments.
    c. power hierarchies.
    d. disengagement.

97. A 16-year-old boy is acting out in ways that are regularly disruptive of the family's home life and social relationships. It soon becomes clear to the social worker that he feels misunderstood, unappreciated, and isolated from much of the family. To encounter this, the social worker asks each of the other family members, "Why do you think he is behaving in these ways?" This is an example of Mara Selvini Palazzoli's Milan Systemic Therapy known as:

    a. hypothesizing.
    b. counter-paradox.
    c. positive connotation.
    d. circular questioning.

98. In community organizing, the fundamental client is:

    a. individual community members.
    b. institutional community members.
    c. the community itself.
    d. informal community organizations.

99. A community member approaches a social worker/community organizer and reveals that a Latino factory owner has been hiring illegal immigrants and then denying them basic breaks and overtime benefits while threatening them with reporting and deportation. In seeking change, the FIRST step the citizen is encouraged to take is as a:

    a. negotiator.
    b. whistleblower.
    c. litigant.
    d. protestor.

100. In pursuing change for individuals or a community, potential social work roles include of the following EXCEPT:

    a. client advocate.
    b. legal advisor.
    c. mediator.
    d. broker.

101. Given that social workers are generally trained to work with voluntary clients (e.g., those who come seeking help), it can be difficult to work with involuntary (e.g., court or employment ordered) clients. Common mechanisms of resistance by involuntary clients include all of the following EXCEPT:

    a. aggression.
    b. diversion.
    c. humor.
    d. withdrawal.

102. The primary objective of supervision is:

    a. keeping the agency running.
    b. meeting the clients' individual needs.
    c. developing the supervisee's skills.
    d. making sure that work is completed.

103. The purpose of clinical/professional consultation in an agency is to:

a. share expertise.
b. obtain alternate leadership.
c. receive direction.
d. defer to an expert.

104. The concept of productive conflict management is drawn from which of the following types of management theories?

a. Bureaucratic
b. Administrative
c. Participative
d. Structuralist

105. A method of program evaluation that examines the extent to which goals are achieved and how well the outcomes can be generalized to other settings and populations is known as:

a. cost-benefit analysis.
b. formative program evaluation.
c. summative program evaluation.
d. peer review.

106. A client is being treated for anxiety but reports having difficulty concentrating on schoolwork and tasks because of being unable to stop worrying. The client has been sleeping poorly and has lost weight. Which complementary therapeutic approach should the social worker advise FIRST?

a. Music therapy
b. Yoga
c. Relaxation exercises
d. Meditation

107. Each state's Division of Child and Family Services (DCFS) commonly provides all of the following services EXCEPT:

a. Child Protective Services.
b. domestic violence shelters.
c. employment training.
d. education referrals.

108. At a transitional family shelter, a newly arrived mother and her three children are being reviewed during an interdisciplinary team consultation. The team consists of the social worker, a housing specialist, and an education and employment specialist. The mother lost her job in another city and was attempting to find work in a larger city. They were living in her car when it was burgled of all possessions. All seem unwell and congested. The oldest child, a 4-year-old boy, has severe asthma and needs a sheltered setting. The 3-year-old girl seems expressively vacant and emotionally detached. The 9-month-old female infant is clearly hungry and lacks diapers and other basic necessities. Food is being obtained for them all. Prior to presenting to the agency director, the FIRST social work step should be to:

    a. complete a psychosocial assessment for mental health issues.
    b. inquire about the availability of extended family support.
    c. obtain clean, warmer clothing from a local clothes closet.
    d. promptly refer the asthmatic boy to a medical doctor.

109. The case recording/progress record acronym SOAP stands for:

    a. Subjective, Overview, Analysis, Prognosis.
    b. Subjective, Observation, Acuity, Proposal.
    c. Subjective, Objective, Assessment, Plan.
    d. Subjective, Orientation, Acceptance, Posits.

110. The service delivery model used by the social worker focuses on helping the client to deal with current behavior in social interactions with a goal of the client's exhibiting behavior that is more acceptable to others so that the client receives positive feedback, further encouraging a change in behavior. Which of the following service delivery models does this exemplify?

    a. Learning/Education
    b. Ecological
    c. Medico-clinical
    d. Social functioning

111. The social worker is on the committee to update the policy and procedure manual for the healthcare organization based on a negative accreditation finding. Other members of the committee have suggested a number of different policies, but the social worker is concerned that the development of policies is not being adequately considered. Which should be the FIRST step in policy development?

    a. Brainstorming different policies
    b. Reviewing other policy and procedure manuals
    c. Identifying problems
    d. Asking for guidance from the board of directors

112. The social worker is in charge of an outreach program that is its own cost center. The organization utilizes a zero-based approach to departmental budgets, and the budget period is coming to an end. Which of the following is the most appropriate action for the social worker?

    a. Wait to see if a budget for the program is allocated
    b. Request that budget be provided based on previous needs
    c. Prepare a report on the benefits of the program and projected budget needs
    d. Expect that the same budget will be provided for the upcoming year

113. Social work ethics may best be defined as:
   a. standards of nonmaleficence.
   b. key professional values.
   c. conduct standards based on values.
   d. standards of beneficence.

114. The ethical concept of Self-Determination refers to:
   a. the right to do anything one wants to do.
   b. the right to require others to help one achieve goals.
   c. the right to make choices dangerous to others.
   d. the right to personal autonomy and decision making.

115. All of the following relate to the concept of confidentiality EXCEPT:
   a. the lack of signage on a substance abuse treatment facility.
   b. installing password protections on clinical computers.
   c. sharing client information only with written permission.
   d. guarding against discussing a client in a public place.

116. In treating a client, the social worker discovers that she had been sexually involved with her last licensed social work therapist. Further questioning revealed that the therapeutic relationship was terminated specifically to allow a relationship, and that sexual contact did not occur until a full year had elapsed after the termination. The client seems fine with how things were handled, and cites her right to confidentiality in an effort to ensure the social worker will not report the issue, even adding that she would deny the information if asked. The BEST response to the information would be to:
   a. ignore it as they are consenting adults, she's no longer his client, and the client has cited confidentiality and intent to deny it.
   b. double-check state laws to see how much time must elapse after termination of a client status before a relationship is possible.
   c. consult with the supervisor or legal counsel to ensure a proper response to the situation.
   d. note the NASW ban on all relationships with clients, current and former, and report, but keep the client's name confidential.

117. A client approaches his social work therapist and asks to see his case files. However, the therapist is concerned that exposure to some sensitive parts of the case record would be harmful to the client. Therefore, the MOST appropriate response to this request would be to:
   a. Refuse, as the case records are the property of the social worker or the agency
   b. Refuse, as the case records are the property of the agency
   c. Allow the review, but with assistance to understand sensitive notes
   d. Allow only a partial review, withholding portions deemed too sensitive

118. During a couple's therapy session they approach a social worker about their 3-year-old daughter's intensely frightening dreams at night. At first it sounds like they are discussing nightmares, but then the social worker recognizes the symptoms as *sleep terrors* (also known as *night terrors* or *pavor nocturnus*). They ask for advice on how to manage the symptoms. As a fully licensed social worker, but with no significant pediatric sleep disorder experience, the BEST response would be to:

    a. refer the child to a counselor with experience in pediatric sleep disorders.
    b. tell the family you will get back with them after doing some research.
    c. complete a quick Internet search and offer a printout of reputable material.
    d. set up an appointment to see the child, and consult a colleague on the issue.

119. The social worker who works in a program for homeless youth is concerned that the need for assistance is much greater than the resources available and is interested in engaging in fundraising to provide an increased budget for the program. What is the FIRST step in fundraising?

    a. Develop budget for fundraising
    b. Establish a goal for fundraising
    c. Determine the target population for fundraising
    d. Define the purpose of the fundraising

120. A client has a concern that warrants consultation. A consulting therapist has expertise in the required area. The BEST way to secure the consult is to:

    a. share the problem and leave the file with the coworker for review.
    b. ask the coworker to review the file, especially recent notes, and offer direction.
    c. set up a formal consultation appointment to discuss the issue(s) in the office.
    d. discuss the concern with the coworker in the cafeteria over lunch.

121. A social worker becomes aware that her colleague has a substance abuse problem. It has become increasingly severe over time, to the extent that the colleague occasionally shows up after lunch breaks clearly compromised and under the influence. The FIRST responsibility of the social worker in this situation is to:

    a. contact a supervisor and report the problem internally.
    b. contact the licensing board and report the problem.
    c. contact the colleague and discuss treatment options.
    d. contact local law enforcement to have them intervene.

122. A social worker discovers that his agency is not following the NASW Code of Ethics as related to secure recordkeeping. In particular, file cabinets are not kept locked, laptop computers used in the field are not password protected, and local university students are regularly permitted to sit in on group therapy sessions without the agreement of group participants and without securing commitments of confidentiality from them. The BEST social work response would be to:

    a. tender a resignation rather than work outside the NASW's standards.
    b. seek to bring the agency's policies and procedures into compliance.
    c. refuse to work with those resources and conditions outside compliance.
    d. none of the above.

123. In the shared governance model used by an organization, each department has autonomous decision- making regarding issues that directly apply to that department, and the leader of each department is also a member on the administrative council. The social worker is interested in making a major change in procedures that involve more than one department. What should be the social worker's FIRST step?

    a. Make a formal proposal to all departments involved regarding the change
    b. Make a formal proposal to the social work department regarding the change
    c. Make a formal proposal to the administrative council, which represents all departments
    d. Discuss the proposal with members of the different departments to build consensus

124. A social worker has been working with homeless clients for many months and has begun to feel mentally and physically exhausted and overwhelmed by encountering the same problems over and over again. The social worker doubts his ability to continue to care for his clients. If these feelings are consistent with compassion fatigue, how is the social worker likely to respond to clients?

    a. With numbness toward their suffering and blaming them for their problems
    b. With compassion and empathy toward their problems
    c. With anger and contempt toward their problems and life choices
    d. With increasing disinterest and apathy toward their problems

125. The presence of a strong therapeutic relationship is fundamental to making positive life changes. Among the most important features of a meaningful therapeutic bond is:

    a. compassion.
    b. empathy.
    c. sympathy.
    d. condolence.

126. In a conversation with a case manager she describes some of her caseload as consisting of "numerous schizophrenics, several bipolars, and some borderlines," after which she proceeds to discuss some of the unique challenges the caseload presents. A primary problem with describing a caseload in this way is that it:

    a. depersonalizes the clients.
    b. stereotypes the clients.
    c. diminishes the clients.
    d. all of the above.

127. In situations of long-term case management, clients should be encouraged to openly share their emotions and feelings. All of the following are benefits to this sharing EXCEPT:

    a. allowing judgment of how acceptable or not the feelings are.
    b. reducing the emotional burdens the client feels.
    c. offering insights into the client's emotional state and coping.
    d. helping the client and worker to see problems more clearly.

128. A social worker is a case manager for a 26-year-old man with a diagnosis of paranoid schizophrenia. In seeking to allow him to ventilate feelings, the client taps into a reservoir of anger about the board and care facility where he resides, and about the operator and his co-residents. His emotions begin to escalate quickly, and a marked sense of lability is present. The BEST response is to:

    a.   confront him about his anger and label it as inappropriate.

    b.   join him in expressing anger and frustration about his situation.

    c.   evaluate him for homicidality and the possible need for intervention.

    d.   seek to understand his feelings while soothing/deescalating them.

129. When offering a client short-term and/or very narrow services, the best way to handle client's expression of feelings is to:

    a.   encourage the deep expression of feelings.

    b.   limit the expression of intense or deep feelings.

    c.   refuse to communicate about feelings in any way.

    d.   none of the above.

130. The social worker can only make one more visit during the workday but has four clients in need of visits, so some visits will have to be made the following day:

- A 2-year-old girl who was placed with a foster parent 5 months previously
- A 12-year-old boy who has repeatedly run away from his foster home
- A 16-year-old girl who is in an emergency room after being raped
- A 14-year old boy who is hospitalized after a recent suicide attempt

Which client should the social worker visit FIRST?

    a.   2-year-old girl in foster care

    b.   12-year-old-boy who repeatedly runs away

    c.   16-year-old girl who was raped

    d.   14-year old boy who recently attempted suicide

131. There are circumstances in which clients reveal a significant role in producing the situation they find themselves in (e.g., addiction, criminal behavior, violence). In such circumstances the FIRST role of the social worker is to:

    a.   point out important societal standards and expectations.

    b.   cite relevant legal and moral standards and expectations.

    c.   ensure a nonjudgmental attitude, regardless of the client's past.

    d.   discuss the consequences of choices and the need for change.

132. A social worker is contracted to work in a probation-sponsored drug rehabilitation setting with court-mandated clients. The program has an information release form that specifies the release of "any relevant information" to "any interested party" for "any requested purpose" without termination date. Staff explain that, given the clientele, information must at times be released to legal authorities or others on an urgent basis, making this broad form necessary. The safety of the public or others could be at stake. The proper social work response would be to:

    a.   use the form as directed, given the circumstances.

    b.   use the form, but note concerns with administration.

    c.   meet with administration to address the use of the form.

    d.   refuse to use the form on grounds that it is unethical.

133. Exceptions to Confidentiality and Release of Information requirements include all of the following EXCEPT:

   a. in situations of actively expressed suicidal ideation.
   b. when a law enforcement official formally requests information.
   c. where a client leads a social worker to suspect harm to others.
   d. where a client discloses abuse to a minor or dependent adult.

134. Confidentiality is BEST managed in group counseling sessions by:

   a. telling participants that confidentiality cannot be assured.
   b. committing group members to keep confidentiality.
   c. having group members sign confidentiality agreements.
   d. all of the above.

135. A social worker at a community counseling agency receives a subpoena to testify in court about one of her clients. The information outlined in the subpoena includes information that could easily be psychologically damaging to her client. The BEST response to this subpoena would be to:

   a. comply with the subpoena, as no other options exist.
   b. refuse to testify, even if contempt of court charges could result.
   c. request the court withdraw the order, or limit its scope.
   d. none of the above.

136. In situations of the death of either the client or the social worker, confidentiality agreements:

   a. remain in full force and effect.
   b. become null and void.
   c. pass on to family members and/or the holder of the client's records.
   d. remain in effect for the client, but not for but not the social worker's records.

137. In working with a client, the social worker discovers him to be manipulative, confrontational, at times deceptive, and otherwise very difficult to work with. Over time the social worker finds it increasingly difficult to work with him, and struggling to contain anger and even expressions of contempt. Concerned that she may not be able to maintain therapeutic clarity and requisite positive regard to support the change process, the social workers FIRST step should be to:

   a. refer him to another social worker.
   b. share these feelings with the client.
   c. seek supervision and/or consultation.
   d. ignore the problem, as it may improve.

138. A social worker is providing counseling services to a Southeast Asian family. After several sessions, the family presents her with a gift of a carefully crafted piece of folk art that they produced themselves. Although the materials involved are of little value, the overall value of the handcrafted item is unclear. In this situation, the social worker should FIRST:

   a. explore the meaning of the gift with the family.
   b. accept the gift graciously, but cite ethical standards for the future.
   c. reluctantly accept the gift, expressing ethical uncertainty.
   d. decline the gift while citing ethical standards as the reason.

139. A social worker provides services to an auto mechanic. At one point the social worker required auto repair work, and the client offered to perform the work in lieu of direct payment for services. The BEST response to this would be to:

    a. accept the request, as it offers mutual advantages.
    b. accept the offer, but set clear boundaries.
    c. decline the offer, suggesting the need for boundaries.
    d. decline the offer, citing professional ethics.

140. The social worker realizes that few staff members are able to leave work on time because of the need for extensive paperwork, and a quality assurance review finds that paperwork is often incomplete. In reviewing the documents required, the social worker notes a number of redundancies and believes that changing the document formats to eliminate redundancies would save considerable time. What should the social worker do FIRST?

    a. Ask the other staff members to help design new documents
    b. Suggest the supervisor consider revising documents
    c. Do a mockup of revised documents and take to the supervisor
    d. Complain to the supervisor that documentation is inefficient

141. A hospice social worker has had an extended relationship with a terminally ill client and his family. After the client's death, the family extends an invitation to attend the funeral and a family-only luncheon following the service. In this situation the BEST response by the social worker would be to:

    a. decline to attend either the funeral or the luncheon.
    b. decline the funeral invitation, but attend the luncheon.
    c. attend the funeral, but decline the luncheon invitation.
    d. attend both the funeral and the luncheon as invited.

142. The social worker has a 16-year-old client who is morbidly obese and expresses shame and anxiety about the weight and her body shape. The client is able to lose a few pounds but invariably then engages in binge-eating and regains the weight that is lost plus additional weight. This causes the client to feel increasingly worthless. Which of the following should the social worker focus on FIRST?

    a. The triggers that result in binge-eating
    b. The client's feelings about body image
    c. Dieting strategies for weight loss
    d. The client's goal for weight loss

143. Social work communication is facilitated through meaningful client questioning. Questions that possess the underlying goal of securing client agreement are known as:

    a. leading questions.
    b. stacked questions.
    c. open-ended questions.
    d. close-ended questions.

144. A social worker is seeing a client under mandatory court orders following conviction for a protracted period of sexual offenses with a minor. In the dialogue process, the client repeatedly refers to her offenses as "a mistake I made" and "when that happened," as well as, "he said he wanted it" and "he kept coming back for more," even after repeatedly being redirected. Recognizing that planned behavior does not just "happen mistakenly" and that a minor can never consent to such behavior, the MOST appropriate therapeutic response would be:

    a. empathic responding.
    b. reflective listening.
    c. confrontation.
    d. none of the above.

145. The concept of *transference* is BEST defined as:

    a. an effort to shift blame for one's own wrongdoing from oneself to another individual.
    b. an emotional reaction toward another, drawn from prior experiences with someone else.
    c. the awareness of how an individual's appearance, mannerisms, language, or behaviors is a reminder of someone difficult from one's past.
    d. a social worker's feeling about a client based upon prior experiences from the social worker's own background.

146. A parent appears to have good communication with his child and shows much warmth and affection but imposes few limits and very little guidance, believing that children should develop "naturally." As a result, the child tends to run wild and has been expelled from two different preschools because of refusal to cooperate. What type of behavior in childhood commonly results from this type of parenting?

    a. Bullying, aggressive, and rebellious behavior
    b. Destructive and delinquent behavior
    c. Passive and needy or aggressive behavior
    d. Independent and capable behavior

147. There are two forms of counseling records that can be kept by a social worker. They are generally referred to by three different titles (two common titles for one, and one for the other). All of the following titles may be used EXCEPT:

    a. the primary client record.
    b. the clinical/medical record.
    c. journal notes.
    d. psychotherapy notes.

148. A client has annual major depression events briefly accompanied by psychotic features. This has resulted in a misdiagnosis of bipolar disorder with psychotic features. The case manager notes that decompensation always occurs in the same month (the anniversary date of the death of her children in a car she was driving), and eventually discovers the misdiagnosis. In attempting to correct the problem, she is coached to leave it unchanged as the client's insurance will not cover the agency's services for a major depression diagnosis. The BEST social work response to this dilemma is to:

    a. leave the diagnosis unchanged, as it was made by a psychiatrist.
    b. leave the diagnosis unchanged to preserve client services.
    c. seek supervision and/or consultation to explore the issue further.
    d. change the diagnosis to properly reflect the client's condition.

149. A social worker has been working with a client for 18 months and the client's problem has been fully addressed and resolved. An appropriate process of termination has been concluded and all services have been discontinued. The state has no prevailing statute for a period of retention for social work records. The client's record should now NEXT be:

    a. destroyed.
    b. thinned and only essential information retained.
    c. kept intact for another 3 years.
    d. retained in accordance with state medical record statutes.

150. A social worker in a genetics clinic is employed to help families given difficult news about their own genetic makeup, or that of their children or unborn children. Part of the counseling process involves the discussion of abortion for fetuses that might otherwise be born with a variety of impairments, ranging from relatively mild to severe. The social worker at times feels distressed by offering the option of abortion in cases of only mild fetal defects. Her BEST response in such situations would be to:

    a. help the family explore their feelings about the defects, their family circumstances, and the meaning of available options.
    b. present all options to the family in a dispassionate and officious manner.
    c. discuss the sanctity of life and how essential it is to preserve it.
    d. help the family understand how manageable it would be to raise a child with only mild defects.

Answer Key and Explanations

1. D: This response represents an example of concrete operational thought. The client is demonstrating a very "concrete" and tangible-focused interpretation of the concept presented. Other key features of concrete operations include decentration (moving from an egocentric perspective to a view centered within a larger world view), reversibility, and manipulation of the steps of a process to achieve determined ends. Sensorimotor interpretation refers to the limited use of physical senses and movement to evaluate the world. Preoperational thought allows for the use of objects in representation (a stick as a sword, etc.), without the ability to logically reason or interpret with insight. Formal operations reflect the ability to reason through hypothetical and abstract concepts. Jean Piaget proposed four stages of cognitive development, noting specifically that some people do not develop past the concrete operational stage even in adulthood. Whether this client has regressed from formal operational thinking to concrete operational thinking, as a symptom of dementia, can be assessed by obtaining a history of his prior cognitive functioning. If so, such regression could represent an early symptom of cognitive impairment.

2. B: William James (1875) researched the function of consciousness as opposed to structure. Other early theorists, in order of theory construction, include the following: Wilhelm Wundt (1873): Structuralism (term coined by his student, Edward Titchener: examining the structure, not the function, of the conscious mind; Wundt is considered the "father of Experimental Psychology"); Sigmund Freud (1900) – Psychoanalytic Theory of Personality; Alfred Adler (1917) – Individual Psychology (birth order, personality development, self-image, etc.); John B. Watson (1920) – Behaviorism (conducted the "Little Albert" experiment, and focused on observable behavior as opposed to mental or emotional states); Ivan Pavlov (1927) – Classical or Respondent Conditioning (experimenting with dogs); Jean Piaget (1928) – Cognitive Development (producing a four-stage developmental model); Lev Vygotsky (1934) – Child Development and Social Development Theory (focused on language in learning processes); Kurt Lewin (1935) – Social Psychology (as well as applied psychology and organizational management); and Anna Freud (1936) – Ego Defense Mechanisms.

3. A: Lawrence Kohlberg (1958) researched the moral reasoning development and produced a six-stage moral judgment model. Other later theorists who focused on human development and behavior include Abraham Maslow (1943) – Hierarchy of Needs (producing a pyramid model of human needs, founded on those most basic and progressing to higher-order needs); Rene Spits (1945) – Ego Development (focused on maternal-child relationships, and identified a form of "hospitalism" called "anaclitic depression"); Erik Erikson (1950) – Ego Psychology (produced a psychosocial developmental model encompassing birth to death); Margaret Mahler (1950) – Separation-Individuation (studied maternal-infant interaction, and created a model of developmental stages from birth through 4 years); B.F. Skinner (1953) – Operant Conditioning (modifying behavior through consequences); John Bowlby and Mary Ainsworth (1969) – Attachment Theory (the psychological impact of losing important attachment figures—typically the mother); Elisabeth Kübler-Ross (1969) – Death and Dying (identified five grief stages when confronting death); Carol Gilligan (1982) – Feminist Social Psychology (studied gender differences); and, James Karl and Karen Wandrei (1990s) – Person in Environment System (PIE) Theory.

4. A: James felt cognitive processing precedes emotions, while Wundt felt that emotions emerge prior to cognitive understanding. Wilhelm Wundt, *the father of experimental psychology*, posited a *structural* view of human consciousness. He focused on exploring the basic structures of the mind, and the subsequent elements of feeling and sensation that constitute consciousness. From this structural perspective, his research experiments in Liepzig, Germany, utilized a technique called *Introspection*, wherein research subjects were provided an experience and then asked to report their feelings and emotional responses. He did not foresee subconscious or unconscious elements in the mind, and thus his experiments were centered on exploration of the conscious mind. William James, *the American father of experimental psychology*, believed that the *functions* of consciousness were more significant and adaptive than the involved *structures*. Consequently, his work at Harvard University focused on how thoughts and behaviors (mental states) serve a functional role in individual adaptation to the environment.

5. D: Preconscious thoughts can be brought to awareness relatively easily, while unconscious thoughts are much more difficult to bring to awareness. Both forms of thought, feeling and ideas, however, actively influence emotions and behaviors and thus must be accounted for in exploring human thinking and behavioral dynamics. Distressing ideas and experiences (i.e., that produce negative feelings and/or responses from others) may be *repressed* and pushed out of the conscious mind into the unconscious realm. Repressed experiences, thoughts, and ideas can exert considerable influence on human behavior. Substantial levels of distress from repression can produce psychological or even physiological dysfunction (e.g., emotional and somatic complaints). Treatment focuses on delving into and bringing repressed thoughts and ideas back to awareness, tracing the associated symptoms, and re-living the troubling experiences and situations in such a way as to produce constructive resolution. Freud's *Psychoanalytic Theory of Personality* addressed: structure of personality, psychosexual stages of child development, and levels of consciousness. Treatment techniques include *free association* and *dream analysis*.

6. C: The driving force is the Id, and the most effective intervention would be to cite the negative consequences of the behavior (arrest, punishment, etc.). Freud postulated three personality structures: 1) the *Id* (pleasure-seeking without regard to others needs or wants); 2) the *Ego* (reality-based, seeking needs in socially appropriate ways); and, 3) the *Superego* (morality based and conscience-driven, replacing the role of parents). This client is still living through the Id, and thus will respond most immediately to the threat or imposition of consequences. While most immediately effective, this has poor long-term influence. Next steps will involve teaching prosocial rules through logical cause-and-effect analysis and understanding (Ego development), ultimately followed by Superego development (teaching empathy and insight into the needs of others, the role of community solidarity and collective contributions to the shared social good, etc.). The Superego includes: a) the *conscience* (the "should nots" of behaviors) and b) the *ego ideal* (the "shoulds" that lead to rewards such as personal esteem and self-dignity and pride). *Life instinct* (Eros) refers to energy (libido) driving basic survival, pleasure, and reproductive needs.

7. D: This client may have a fixation in the Oral Stage. Freud suggested that fixation in the oral stage (the first year) might emerge in cases of infant neglect (inadequate feeding) or overprotection (excessive feeding). The mother's breast (or a substitute) becomes an early object of cathexis (emotional attachment). Thus, a neglected child may become a manipulative adult, seeking to compensate for the neglect, and an overprotected child may regress to untoward dependence upon others. In theory, oral-stage fixations become evident in various oral stimulus needs (eating, chewing on things, garrulousness, alcoholism, smoking, etc.). The Anal Stage (2-3 years of age) is not relevant, as it manifests in preoccupation with bowel and bladder functions. The Phallic Stage (3-6 years of age) involves genital discovery and pleasure, as well as mastery of Oedipal or Electra Complexes, which are unrelated to this situation. The Latency Period (6-11 years of age) is not relevant as it focuses on work and play with same-sex friends, with fixation here resulting in later untoward discomfort with opposite-sex relationships. Finally, the Genital Stage (age 12 to adulthood) would not apply as it occurs with puberty, and a return to opposite sex interests.

8. C: Birth order and guiding fiction would best explain their situation, according to the Adlerian perspective. While opposites may attract, mismatching can be complicated. Adler characterized the youngest as potentially dependent and spoiled, and potentially willing to manipulate others into caregiving and support. An oldest, by contrast, tends to be focused on responsibility and control. Both are evident in their conflicts. Further, the spouse's need for a superordinate work position suggests Adler's *guiding fiction* (an internally created self-image, never fully congruent with reality) is dysfunctionally present, where childhood feelings of inferiority compel him to find success beyond immediate experience or capacity and to shun any perceived menial work. *Needs hierarchy* is not Adlerian, as it was developed by Maslow, nor is it applicable here. Ego and superego are not relevant, as Adler did not accept these Freudian constructs. Inferiority and superiority issues are evident, but these concepts do not provide an optimal paradigm from which to pursue treatment.

9. D: John B. Watson, an American psychologist, developed the concept of *Behaviorism*, which consisted of an objective method of analyzing the cause and effect of identified behaviors. In exploring behavior, he conducted the "Little Albert" experiment in which a child was taught to fear a white rabbit—not because of anything the rabbit did, but because of overprotective parental anxiety and chastisement. The initial target of Little Albert's fear was a white rat, but it was readily generalized to a white rabbit. In like manner, this child's fear of going outdoors and certain home situations gradually expanded to a great many other social situations. Both Skinner and Pavlov were behavioral theorists, but both also focused primarily on direct stimulus-response conditioning (action-consequence links), as opposed to the expanded generalized conditioning that was the focus of Watson's Behaviorism. Jean Piaget studied cognitive development as opposed to behavioral conditioning. Thus, Piaget could better describe the cognitive threshold required for such complex associations to be made, as opposed to the behavioral conditioning that could produce it.

10. D: This compulsion would be described as a conditioned response. The word "Pavlovian" refers to the theoretical work of Ivan Pavlov. An unconditioned stimulus is one that evokes an innate unconditioned response (i.e., a startle reflex at a loud noise). A conditioned stimulus is one that produces a learned response, because it has been paired with an unconditioned stimulus in the past (e.g., a rush of elation when your football team scores a touchdown—two experiences that would have no real meaning or response until they were paired and learned). The classic example is that of Ivan Pavlov's research with dogs. Presented with meat powder, the dogs would salivate. Eventually, a bell was added at the point of presentation of the meat powder. Ultimately the dogs would salivate at the sound of the bell alone, without any meat powder. Thus, an unconditioned stimulus and response, when paired with another stimulus, eventually became a learned stimulus with a learned response.

11. B: The human development theorist Lev Vygotsky focused his research primarily on child development, and introduced a concept later known as *scaffolding*. His original concept, called the *Zone of Proximal Development* (ZPD), explains how a child functions at a lower limit if all help is withheld, and moves to a higher level with skilled assistance. *Scaffolding* is an extension of ZPD. It refers to a teaching pattern where an adult provides more intensive assistance to a child at the outset of learning a difficult task, and then tapers back as greater skill is acquired. A professional driving instructor uses a teaching vehicle with two steering wheels and two brake pedals, which allows for a measured transition between teaching and allowing the new driver to gradually assume full control. Scaffolding is not possible in a vehicle lacking these tools. Behavior modification may be helpful in extinguishing a persistent bad driving habit, but not in optimizing initial training. Defense mechanisms may explain the daughter's inability to learn from dad, but not the path to learning. Anaclitic depression is a concept from attachment theory with no bearing on this situation.

12. B: This older adult has suffered multiple losses and may feel she has lost control of her life, so exhibiting oppositional behavior is her way of reasserting control. The social worker should listen actively to the woman's complaints in a non-judgmental manner, encouraging her to express her feelings. Then, the social worker should suggest they collaborate to devise a personal schedule of activities, explaining why some things can't be changed (meal times, scheduled activities) and encouraging choice in other things (bathing, room cleaning). After this, the social worker should counsel the staff but should avoid telling the woman that her behavior is inappropriate.

13. C: This is an example of intellectualization. Specifically, *intellectualization* occurs when an individual attempts to use logic and reasoning to avoid facing difficult feelings. As with many other defense mechanisms, this coping effort is not necessarily problematic as it may offer the spouse a place of refuge until he is psychologically ready to encounter the devastating feelings that it is covering. Thus, this need should be recognized and accommodated unless it becomes unduly protracted and/or exclusive of gradual exploration of the underlying emotional concerns. *Projection* addresses the denial of one's own negative characteristics while attributing them to someone else (e.g., "I'm not a racist! You should see what my mom says about foreigners!"). *Compensation* refers to success seeking in one life area to substitute for barriers in another that cannot or have not been overcome. Rationalization involves hiding one's actual motivations under an appeal to more socially acceptable reasoning and logic (e.g., saying "I can't make the trip because the kids are sick," instead of admitting you don't enjoy the people or activity).

14. B: The defense mechanism known as *fixation* refers to arrested personality development at a stage short of normative maturation. This client clearly identifies with individuals and activities that fall short of her age and maturity level. While enjoying youthful associations is not in itself problematic, seeking to live in those associations to the exclusion of normal relationships and activities is problematic. Identifying, addressing, and overcoming the reasons behind this will likely be a major therapeutic endeavor. *Avoidance* is characterized by a refusal to become involved with objects, situations, and/or activities that are related to underlying impulses to avoid potential punishment (e.g., staying away from casinos to cope with a predilection for gambling instead of discovering and overcoming the underlying reasons for the compulsion). *Devaluation* involves the attribution of negative qualities to oneself or others to cope with stress or internal emotional conflicts (e.g., coping with being fired from a job by speaking negatively of the job and work colleagues). *Affiliation* involves seeking emotional support and advice from others instead of "going it alone," yet without trying to make others responsible to step in and fix the problem.

15. C: The best response is to permit some discussion on feelings of loss, but keep the focus on his immediate housing, transportation, and employment needs. Abraham Maslow's Needs Hierarchy posits that more essential and basic physiological needs must be met before higher order needs. Thus, needs regarding food, clothing, and shelter are more important than needs for safety (security, protection, predictability, and structure), belonging (friendships, affection, intimacy), esteem (recognition, respect, and appreciation), and self-actualization (meeting one's full potential). Thus, while it is important to acknowledge and make some room for the client's feelings of grief and loss, it is crucial that more basic survival needs be met first. Just "going where the client wants to be" is clinically irresponsible. Rejecting all talk about relationships and loss would be alienating, and referring him away would be abandoning him without the support that is available through the agency.

16. C: This client is struggling with the mastery of Erikson's Stage 6: intimacy vs. isolation. This stage is typically mastered during young adulthood (ages 19-30). Indicators of successful resolution include establishing a committed, intimate, nonexploitive sexual relationship, with meaningful tolerance for the burdens and risks that accompany the relationship. The client has not been able to establish a reciprocal, loving, intimate relationship with another individual. The sexual relationships that he has produced are transient, noncommittal, and often exploitive. Failure to negotiate this stage results in increasing isolation and narcissism. A, Stage 1 (trust vs. mistrust), is not correct as the issue of failures in trust has not been identified. B, Stage 5 (identity vs. identify diffusion), is not correct, as the client does not present with issues related to roles and self-identity. D, Stage 8 (integrity vs. despair) is not correct, as this is an end-of-life construct dealing with self-assessment in retrospect and the client is not at this point in life.

17. D: This disorder likely occurs from problematic experiences in Mahler's Stage 3: Rapprochement. *Rapprochement* is one of four substages in Stage 3 of Mahler's child development model. During this substage, an infant (15-24 months of age) begins to strive for autonomy. Success requires maternal support, as the infant ventures away from immediate contact, and frequently returns for encouragement and assurances of security. Where these are not forthcoming, an infant can develop anxiety and fears of abandonment. This can evolve into a dysfunctional *mood predisposition* that, Mahler felt, could later produce Borderline and/or Narcissistic Personality traits or the full disorder. Answer A (normal autism phase) is not correct, as it refers to a natural obliviousness to the external world common from birth to 1 month. Answer B (symbiosis phase) refers to high levels of attachment between mother and infant from 1-4 months of age, with deprivation/disruption potentially resulting in later symbiotic psychosis and disconnection from reality. Answer C (differentiation [hatching] phase) refers to an infant's realization of being separate from its mother. As an awakening, rather than a process, it is does not produce psychological failure.

18. A: The problem would be identified as one of positive reinforcement. The teenager's acting out led to a variety of responses and punishments. However, it is revealed that the teenager's underlying goal is time and attention from her father. As negative attention is better than no attention at all (i.e., *positive reinforcement*), the teenager continued to act out to receive and extend attention from her father. Answer B (*negative reinforcement*) is incorrect, as it refers to the repetition of a desired behavior to avoid negative stimuli (consequences). The parents were supplying negative stimuli (stern lectures) to produce and strengthen positive (cooperative) behaviors. Answer C (*punishment*) was also being used to weaken the teen's use of negative behaviors. Answer D (*extinction*) refers to the weakening of a conditioned response in one of two ways: 1) in *classical (Pavlovian) conditioning*, it involves interrupting the pairing of a conditioned stimulus and an unconditioned stimulus; 2) in *operant conditioning*, it occurs when a trained behavior ceases to be reinforced (or when the reinforcement is no longer considered rewarding). Ignoring bad behavior is one (operant conditioning) way of bringing it to extinction.

19. B: Skinner's *operant conditioning* deals with the modification of voluntary behavior via consequences, while *Pavlovian conditioning* produces behavior under new antecedent conditions. Ivan Pavlov's classical (or respondent) conditioning utilized the identification of an unconditioned (natural) stimulus that evokes an unconditioned response (e.g., food inducing salivation). A conditioned stimulus is created when an unconditioned stimulus is repeatedly paired with a stimulus to be conditioned (e.g., ringing a bell with the presentation of food), which evokes the unconditioned response (salivation), which is gradually transitioned into a conditioned response (salivation at the sound of the bell). Skinner identified an antecedent (stimulus) that could be used to produce a response (behavior) that could be controlled or modified by means of a consequence (positive or negative). Positive and negative reinforcements strengthen targeted behaviors, while punishment and extinction weaken targeted behaviors.

20. B: The husband's level, according to Kohlberg's multisystem model of moral development, would be at Level 2: Stage 4. This stage embodies a law-and-order perspective, focused on adherence to concrete perceptions of correct behavior and duty. Clearly, the husband is intent on ensuring he does not fail in his role as husband and father. To increase marital satisfaction, however, the husband needs to progress beyond Levels 1 and 2, and past Level 3: Stage 5 (societal expectations and agreements) into Stage 6, which is conscience- and ethics-driven according to principles of goodness and morality. Answer A (Level 1: Stage 2) is incorrect as Level 1 (Pre-Conventional Morality) is focused first on a punishment avoidance orientation (Stage 1) and next on a reciprocity, instrumental orientation (Stage 2: "you scratch my back and I'll scratch yours). The husband is beyond these stages. He is also beyond Level 2 (Conventional Morality), which deals with approval seeking (Stage 3: being "good" for praise). Answer C (Level 3: Stage 5) is incorrect, as it refers to behavior that has been carefully examined via a social-contract perspective. Finally, answer D (Level 3: Stage 6, ethics and morality driven) is the desired goal, which has yet to be pursued.

21. B: When assessing a one-year-old child's attachment to her mother, the mother plays with the child and then leaves the room, and the child typically begins to cry. When the mother then returns to the room, the first action by the child that suggests the child is securely attached to the mother is if the child hugs the mother and then calms and usually resumes playing. If the child is not securely attached, the child may act ambivalently toward the mother, may continue to cry and even resist comforting, or may cling fearfully to the mother.

22. D: If the social worker is applying feminist theory to a group of women who are substance abusers and come from a variety of ethnic and social backgrounds, the social worker would stress the commonalities among the women. Feminist theory intends to cast light on issues of discrimination inequality, oppression, objectification, and stereotyping faced by women, regardless of their background. Feminist theory considers not only the individual's ability to function in a situation or deal with a problem but also the social circumstances associated with the situation or problem.

23. D: Childhood psychopathology would most likely become apparent during language development. This developmental period requires mastery of *phonology* (making sounds correctly); *semantics* (the encoding of messages); *syntax* (proper combining of words); and *pragmatics* (proper use of word context). Because of the complexity of language development, some forms of psychopathology (e.g., autism) are more readily apparent in this developmental phase. Irregularities in physical developmental milestones are more likely to identify congenital defects, while poor cognitive development may more readily reveal genetic and drug exposure issues. Sexual development requires careful parenting, to ensure sexual curiosities are properly directed in socially appropriate manners, while also ensuring that emerging sexuality is not "shamed" or otherwise impaired or distorted.

24. C: Failure of an infant to crawl by 12 months would be a cause for concern. On average, from birth to 2 months infants respond to faces and bright objects; by 2 months, most visually track moving objects and exhibit social smiling; by 4 months, cooing sounds are evident as well as enjoyment of important people and familiar objects; by 5 months, grasping and holding skills are observed; by 6 months, babies can turn over and teething begins; around 7 months objects can be picked up; by 8 months sitting independently occurs, and stranger anxiety begins; at 9 months crawling is usually seen; at 10 months active play and paying attention are evident; at 11 months standing can be achieved with help; at 12 months a baby can turn pages to see pictures; from 10-12 months the range of emotional expression broadens, and walking with help begins; by 15 months independent walking starts and naming of familiar objects is evident; by 18 months running is observed; at 24 months speech in short sentences is possible; and by age 6 years speech and imagination are both well demonstrated.

25. D: The most appropriate response would be to reassure the parents that this is not itself a symptom of sexual abuse. Approximately 10% of girls will experience menarche before age 11, most at 12.5 years of age, and 90% by 13.75 years of age. Adolescence is typically identified as the period from 12 to 18 years of age. Sexual maturation may begin as young as age 10. Interest in the opposite gender becomes increasingly prominent as maturation progresses. Adolescent development broadens into areas such as emotional and spiritual awareness and capacity. The period is markedly influenced by factors such as gender, socioeconomic status, culture, genetics, and disabilities. Friends and institutional influences become more significant, and adolescents experiment with a variety of "personality styles" as their self-image is formed. Gender identity and potential confusion may occur and require careful response to avoid psychological distress and accompanying increases in depression, abuse, and suicide. Of all developmental periods, this transitional time is typically the most turbulent and traumatic.

26. C: Sandwich generation refers to the pressure of couples still rearing children while being required to care for aging parents. Other significant pressures in adulthood include: 1) caring for disabled children (whether due to health, substance abuse, or other disability); 2) rearing grandchildren for divorced or otherwise unavailable children; 3) economic challenges and poverty, including difficulties accompanying retirement; and 4) personal health changes related to aging. Early to-mid-adulthood is characterized by a focus on dating, marriage, home establishment, and childbearing and rearing. Early family structure can be particularly compromised by physical and/or mental illness, divorce or widowhood (with the accompanying financial, emotional, and social changes), and poor parenting skills (often derived from family of origin). The availability of social work resources can help mitigate the impact of these stressors and challenges. Late-life stressors also include mobility and cognitive changes (e.g., inevitable declines in short-term memory, and the possibility of dementia due to Alzheimer disease, Parkinson disease, stroke).

27. B: The most likely perpetrator in this situation would be the mother. While sexual abuse and/or physical abuse in a child older than 14 years is more likely to be perpetrated by a father or other male father figure in the home, for nonsexual abuse of a child younger than 14 years, the most common perpetrator is the female parent. Common signs of physical abuse include bruising, welts, burns, fractures, and internal injuries. Routine signs of sexual abuse include trouble sitting or walking, inordinate shyness in changing clothes around others, sexual acting out, running away from home, and sexually transmitted diseases. Emotional abuse signs include delays in language skills, distrust, overeagerness to please, insecurity, anxiousness, poor self-esteem, relationship issues, substance abuse, and criminal behavior. Signs of abusive neglect include emotional problems (particularly depression), malnourishment (seen in inhibited development), cognitive delays (due to inadequate stimulation), medical problems and illnesses (especially when left untreated), poor social skills, impaired school performance, poor parental supervision, chronic tardiness or truancy, poor hygiene, and inappropriate clothing.

28. D: The first social worker response should be to contact the local Adult Protective Services (APS) to report suspected abuse. With continued nursing visits, it might be possible to defer a referral if the sole issue is marginal care, while an extended family conference is arranged (option C). However, the withholding of financial resources (the house), as well as isolating and neglecting the client's emotional and nutritional needs, meets clear standards of abuse. Most states have mandatory reporting guidelines when abuse is clear, and the social worker could not ethically or legally withhold the APS referral. Option A is clearly incorrect as it allows the abuse to continue. Option B is not acceptable as it defers any change in the ongoing abuse for at least 2 additional months. Elder abuse includes physical abuse, financial exploitation, and neglect, as well as verbal and emotional abuse, with family being the most common perpetrators. Neglect is the most commonly reported abuse. Living on the client's income and in the client's home are particular risk factors, as are: 1) a difficult to manage client (violent, demented, argumentative, etc.); 2) compromised caregivers (finances, substance abuse, mental illness, etc.); and 3) poor housing (crowded, inadequate, etc.).

29. B: If the social worker is conducting a home evaluation for a client with two children, one neurotypical and the other severely disabled with autism spectrum disorder, and the client admits to being overwhelmed at times and feeling like running away, based on role theory the social worker would describe the client's situation as role strain because the client's stress is related to different aspects of the same status—that of mother. Role conflict arises when conflict arises between different statuses, such as between the role of mother and the role of wife (parts of the client's role set). In some cases, both role conflict and role strain may be present.

30. B: This behavior would best be defined as codependent. Addiction is frequently a family disorder, as it affects all members in the household. Codependent behavior can include making excuses for the addiction, minimizing the extension of the addiction, covering for (or hiding) the addict's behavior, providing access to the substance to keep peace and minimize discord, and bypassing important obligations and responsibilities to compensate for the addict's behaviors and to ensure the safety of the addict or others. Addictions tend to persist because they engage the brain's pleasure center, releasing neurotransmitters that reinforce the addiction. While many addictions involve the use of psychoactive substances, other areas of addiction include eating, shopping, gambling, hoarding, pornography, and the excessive use of electronic devices (computer games, etc.). While most treatment tends to be cognitive behavioral in nature, there are numerous treatment approaches; no one treatment will meet the personality and needs of all addicted individuals.

31. C: These are symptoms of grief bargaining. Drawing upon the work of Kübler-Ross, the social worker recognizes the symptoms of the *bargaining* stage of coping with profound loss. The stages of anticipatory dying were first outlined by the psychiatrist Elisabeth Kübler-Ross. She identified five stages associated with anticipatory grief: *Stage 1: Denial* (rejection of the diagnosis; often a feature of emotional shock). *Stage 2: Anger* (rage, resentment, and frustration with God and others). *Stage 3: Bargaining* (attempting to make a deal with God or others). *Stage 4: Depression* (profound sadness as reality sinks in). *Stage 5: Acceptance* (ceasing to struggle against impending death). Answer A (psychotic break) is not correct, as a psychotic break is symptomatic of a complete detachment from reality, rather than just one deeply distressing element of life. Answer B (chemotherapy toxicity) is inaccurate, as it suggests a chemically driven psychological stage that would be very poorly integrated and lack goal-directed intent. Answer D (acute denial) is not correct, as it would manifest more as a total rejection of the diagnosis, rather than an effort to bargain around it.

32. C: If the social worker has a 10-year-old client who does not appear to be resilient after surviving a traumatic and abusive background, the first step to building resilience in the child is to facilitate a nurturing relationship with an adult. Children who lack resilience are often very fearful and feel unsafe in the world, so they need to identify with an adult who can provide a safe haven, and that can be a parent, family member, or other caring adult. The next step is to provide the child with opportunities to be successful in order to begin to build the child's sense of self-esteem.

33. D: If the social worker wants to conduct research and decides to utilize the conflict theory as the basis for research, the first question that the social worker would pose is "Who most benefits?" Conflict theory is based on the survival of the fittest and the competition for resources and power, resulting in winners and losers, or elite and others. Conflict theory developed from the ideas of Karl Marx and often focuses on issues of inequality.

34. C: Ethnographic interviewing allows for deeper cultural insights to be winnowed out of a client's narratives. Attending to both feelings and cultural meanings, the interviewer is better able to delve into and understand narratives and circumstances from the client's unique perspective. Common listening techniques such as *reframing* and *paraphrasing* are avoided, as they tend to suffuse the narrative with meanings and understandings that reflect the culture and history of the interviewer rather than that of the interviewee. Instead, *restating* and *incorporating* are used to retain the client's unique meanings. The use of an interpreter is important to ensure that unique expressions, such as idioms, or borrowed native-language terms, are not misunderstood or overlooked. Other culturally responsive assessment tools may be helpful. For example, 1) A *Culturagram* can be used to examine family relationships, cultural ties, and offer some perspective about the role and depth of culture in the client's life. 2) A *Cultural Evaluation* may also be used, as it explores a variety of cultural beliefs, values, behaviors, and support systems during the assessment process.

35. A: The *nurturing system* refers to family and intimate supports, while the *sustaining system* refers to institutional supports and society as a whole. As theorists such as Leon Chestang posit, everyone is a part of and in need of both systems of support. Thus, it is essential to understand the roles that culture and diversity play in either furthering or hindering the efficacy and balance of both of these systems in the lives of individuals. In particular is a "dual perspective," which may arise in the lives of culturally diverse clients, wherein they must constantly reposition themselves between nurturing family supports and a broader social construct that may not be in support of the nurturing family's culturally unique ways of living and supporting family members. Discrimination and cultural norms that are incongruent with the broader sustaining system may significantly impede the utilization of important social services in particular.

36. C: In developing a bicultural identity, *assimilation* occurs when the norms and values of the sustaining system (institutions and society) are learned and followed to the exclusion of the norms and values of the nurturing system (family and cultural roots). This division can be particularly problematic among new immigrants and their young offspring. The parents, especially those from highly divergent cultures with markedly different languages and traditions, often find themselves unable to function well in mainstream society. Consequently, they become significantly dysfunctional in the eyes of the children, who far more quickly learn the dominant language and ways. As the parents turn to their young children for help in interpreting and guiding them through systems and technologies, traditional values of respect and reverence for adults can be significantly diminished. *Traditional adaptation* exists where adherence to the nurturing system (family and culture) remains dominant. *Marginal adaptation* occurs when neither the nurturing nor the sustaining systems' values and norms are followed. *Bicultural adaptation* exists when the norms and values of both systems become functionally integrated.

37. D: The null hypothesis for this study would state that there shall be no measurable difference in depression symptom reporting between the control group and the intervention group. The null hypothesis (often designated as "H_0") proposes that no relationship exists between two variables (often designated "x" and "y") other than that arising from chance alone. If a study's results demonstrate no difference, then the null hypothesis is "accepted." If differences emerge, then the study "failed to reject the null hypothesis." Statistical testing does not prove any hypotheses, but instead disproves them via rejection.

38. D: If a 32-year old client living with two adolescent children in a temporary shelter for battered women and their children did not graduate from high school and has never had a job, the client is likely to only qualify for low-paying jobs, which may provide less income than welfare benefits. Realistically, returning to school and attending college would take years, so the best approach to lifting the client from poverty is to enroll the client in a job training program so the client will qualify for a higher paying job.

39. C: This client is still lingering in Stage 6 (withdrawal from the heterosexual world) and Stage 7, as pride and assertiveness about her sexual orientation is still only in its formative processes. The *Coming Out Process* involves 10 Stages: Stage 1: Confusion over sexual identity. Stage 2: Recognition of sexual identity. Stage 3: Exploration relative to sexuality identity (seeking to understand, define, and express sexual identity internally and with others). Stage 4: Disclosure to others. Stage 5: Acceptance of sexual identity. Stage 6: Avoidance of the heterosexual world. Stage 7: Pride in sexual identity. Stage 8: Extending disclosure (to all others). Stage 9: Re-entering the heterosexual world. Stage 10: Moving past sexual orientation (in identity and life focus).

40. A: The term *intersex* refers to ambiguous sexual anatomy (hermaphrodite). Heterosexual orientation is most commonly referred to as being *straight*. There is no specific term for sexual encounters outside of orientation preference. Sexual attraction to both men and women is known as *bisexuality*. Homosexual men are most often referred to as *gay*, while homosexual women are referred to by the term *lesbian*. *Pansexuality* refers to an attraction to and association with any partner regardless of sexual identity. *Transgender* (also called bi-gender) refers to an identity different from birth sex type, with a focus on gender. Transgender individuals may live a heterosexual, homosexual, bisexual, or asexual lifestyle. *Transsexual* individuals have identified themselves as transgender with a focus on sexual orientation. Further, they have an added desire to live an opposite sex lifestyle and desire hormonal and/or sexual surgery to achieve physiological congruence. *Genderqueer* and *Intergender* are catch-all terms for those who feel they are both male and female, neither male nor female, or entirely all binary gender identity.

41. D: The first response should be to refer the client to a primary care physician for a health evaluation. Women are far more likely than men to be diagnosed with a psychiatric disorder, especially a psychogenic disorder of mood, when an underlying medical condition (such as hormone imbalance) is the cause. Seeking parity with men in many areas, including psychiatry, remains a challenge. Culturally, women continue in subordinate positions in society, specifically in medical, legal, and institutional arenas. Problems include 1) psychiatric and medical studies run by men and for men, with findings normed to men (especially in pharmaceutical findings where doses are normed to men's larger size and faster metabolic patterns, and in psychiatric studies that tend to either ignore or pathologize women's unique nature); 2) being uninsured or underinsured (double the rate of men); 3) lower pay for similar work (even worse for female minorities); and 4) poverty (women represent 66% of all Medicaid recipients). Women also fare poorly in intimacy, being far more often abused and more prone to sexual infections (such as HIV). All are also contributors to depression, beyond simple endogenous factors.

42. D: The best response is to key in on the phrase and inquire directly about suicidal thoughts. Elderly people face many challenges, among which is Erikson's *Integrity vs. Despair* resolution process becoming profoundly acute in older years. Among elderly people, losses accumulate, health is fading, children have left, options are narrowing greatly, and the future can easily seem dim. Health and medication problems can further complicate the scenario. Of particular note, while the highest rate of completed suicide is among middle-aged Caucasian men (45 to 64 years old), the second highest rate is among elderly Caucasian men. While women attempt suicide three times as often as men, men are four times more likely to succeed, primarily because they often use more

78

lethal means (firearms, suffocation, etc.). Of all completed suicides, 78.5% are male and 21.5% female. On average, 12 people attempt to harm themselves for every reported death by suicide. Many of these represent gestures rather than real attempts. Elderly persons, however, are decidedly lethal. While the ratio of attempts to completed suicides is 25:1 among youth, it is 4:1 among the elderly. Certainly, it is always important to ask if concerning words are used.

43. A: If the social worker has a special interest in assisting clients who are attempting to move from welfare benefits to the world of work, establishing partnerships with industry to train and employ clients would best indicate that the social worker is actively promoting economic justice. This type of program can help lift clients out of poverty and allow them to earn a living wage. The goal of economic justice is to allow each individual to engage in a productive life.

44. B: Military discipline (assignment changes, rank changes, sanctions, etc.) would not normally contribute to a diagnosis of *Posttraumatic Stress Disorder* (PTSD). Combat stress (battle fatigue) is a primary contributor to PTSD. It includes exposure to experiences of violence and mayhem, and the psychological trauma associated with killing and living under the constant stress of being killed. *Military Sexual Trauma* (MST) is often overlooked in recovering veterans (rates of MST are 22% and 1.2%, respectively), especially if the veteran is male. *Mild traumatic brain injury* (MTBI) is also an often-overlooked contributor. Of note, MTBI does not require loss of consciousness or even a diagnosable concussion to be an issue. Any substantial blow to the head or even close proximity to certain kinds of explosive blasts can bring it on, sometimes immediately and sometimes in a delayed form. They key symptoms are unexplained episodes of confusion, disorientation, loss of concentration, feeling dazed, etc. Neuropsychiatric consultation is important in such situations.

45. B: The NASW position on undocumented immigrants, most recently updated in 2018, is to assist these individuals and families in obtaining rights, services, benefits, education, health care, mental health, and other services whenever possible. Not only does the NASW Code of Ethics direct members to oppose any mandatory reporting by social workers, but to also oppose such requirements by members in other professions such as health, education, mental health, policy makers, and among public service providers. Further, undocumented immigrants are to be recognized as particularly vulnerable to exploitation and abuse, and thus they are to receive advocacy services and all available protections from violence (especially as perpetrated upon women) and other forms of abuse and exploitation. All these services are to be provided in a culturally competent manner.

46. C: Insurance and ability to pay is obviously important, but it is not part of an *Intake Interview*. Rather it is a part of screening for services. Key areas of an intake interview include the following: 1) Problem areas (presenting problem, or chief complaint); common areas include relationships, finances, and psychosocial functioning. 2) Strengths: coping skills, resources, capacities, etc. 3) Support systems: significant others, family, friends, organizations, and affiliations, and their scope of involvement and availability. 3) Attitude: positive and progressive versus defeatist and negative, which may influence treatment. 4) Motivation: direct and clear, or for secondary gain or manipulation (e.g., to placate others, meet legal or employment requirements). 5) Relationships: nature, significance and role in life. 6) Resources: those used previously and others currently available, as well as personal resources (faith, values, cognitive capacity, problem-solving skills, etc.). 7) Danger to self or others: suicidality and homicidality must always be explored if there is any indication of relevance. Important risk factors that might contribute to dangerousness should also be noted.

47. A: If the social worker has increasing numbers of clients who are refugees from third world countries and notes that many exhibit signs of depression but are very resistant to any type of referral to mental health services, denying that they have a problem, the most likely reason for this response is a different attitude toward mental illness. Because there is often a stigma attached to a diagnosis of mental illness, people may consider indications, such as withdrawal, crying, insomnia, and sadness, as simply part of life and not something that requires intervention.

48. B: The *medical model* in health care is focused on the *presenting problem* or *chief complaint*. Thus, when used in mental health, it is focused on clients' complaints, deficits, and identified problems. However, this assessment approach tends to miss identification of a client's positive life features, strengths, resiliency, and motivation. The *strengths perspective* views a client's capacities, internal motivations, and dedication to be essential elements of successful problem resolution, healing, and overcoming. A focus on problems can often disempower a client, leaving them feeling mired and overwhelmed in their challenges. In contrast, the strengths perspective focuses on competencies, capacities, resources, confidence, and alternatives—all of which are empowering, positive, and success focused. The *biopsychosocial model* explores the biological (physical), psychological, and social features that may be contributing to a client's concerns and challenges. It readily accounts for issues of environment, culture, poverty, social status, and health as a relevant constellation in which problems and challenges are embedded. Each model has something valuable to offer, and one or another may be preferable depending upon the clinical purpose, therapeutic goals, and environment (crisis vs. long-term contacts, etc.).

49. C: If an adolescent client in foster care repeatedly complains of various ailments but symptoms usually subside shortly after the client is allowed to stay home from school, suggesting the client is feigning illness, the most appropriate response is, "I can see that you are avoiding school because of something that may be difficult for you to talk about." Directly challenging an adolescent or demanding an explanation is likely to result only in withdrawal, but the social worker should acknowledge the client's feelings and allow the opportunity for sharing.

50. B: The best response is to discuss his concerns and support him, but require the collateral contact. It is important to create a therapeutic bond with the client, but not to the exclusion of collateral contacts that are reasonable. The client should be given every opportunity to discuss his concerns, particularly if the therapy ended badly, and he should feel well heard and supported. Further, some collateral contacts (such as with a bitter ex-spouse) can very understandably be refused, but an extended therapeutic relationship should not be circumscribed by a client, as crucial information could be lost and the therapeutic work be thwarted.

51. C: The first response should be to complete a suicide risk evaluation, and then arrange voluntary hospitalization if the client will accept it. As the client's social worker, it is important to complete a suicide risk evaluation, recognizing that it may be more complete, candid, and factual than what the client might reveal during assessment by an unfamiliar clinician. Given the client's emotional state (deliberate calm), detailed plans, and summary rationale, the client is at very high risk for acting on her suicidal thoughts. Further, she has not only motivation and rationale, but the means and anticipated timing for carrying out her plans. Therefore, even if the client were to recant, hospitalization would still be essential to ensure client safety. Calling 911 immediately would be premature and overly reactive. Calling local law enforcement is also overly reactive, and prevents the client from accepting voluntary hospitalization (as involuntary confinement is traumatic, and may produce unintended legal, social, and emotional consequences). Finally, research suggests that suicide prevention contracting alone tends to be ineffective, though potentially meaningful in early suicidal ideation situations.

52. A: The social worker's duty now is to contact the client's wife to inform her of the danger. According to recent interpretations of the case Tarasoff v. Regents of the University of California

(1976, California Supreme Court ruling) confidentiality, in this situation, may be breeched if 1) the HIV infection is known; 2) unprotected sex (or sharing of needles) is occurring; 3) the behavior is actually unsafe; 4) the client refuses to modify his behavior even after being counseled regarding the harm; and 5) if HIV transmission will likely occur.

53. A: The MSE does NOT cover addictions and compulsions. The domains examined in a Mental Status Examination (MSE) are: alertness (attending) and orientation (to person, place, and time = A&Ox3) appearance (physical presentation, dress, hygiene, grooming, etc.), attitude (e.g., cooperative, hostile, guarded, suspicious), behavior (activity, eye contact, movements, gait, mannerisms, psychomotor agitation or retardation, etc.), mood and affect (euphoric, euthymic, dysphoric, anxious, apathetic, anhedonic, etc.), thought processes (rate, quantity, and form [logical or illogical, rapid, or pressured "flights of ideas," perseveration], etc.), thought content (delusions [with or without ideas of reference], grandiosity, paranoia, erotomanic, insertions, broadcasting, etc.), speech (rate and rhythm, poverty or loquacious, pitch, articulation, etc.), perception (hallucinations [visual, auditory, tactile, gustatory, or olfactory], depersonalization, derealization, time distortion [déjà vu], etc.), cognition (alertness, orientation, attention, fund of information, short- and long-term memory and recall, language, executive functions [tested via interpretations], etc.), insight (understanding of problems and options) and judgment (logically reasoned decisions).

54. D: If an 8-year-old child has an out-of-home placement in a temporary foster home because of severe neglect and abandonment by her parents and reports that she has one younger sibling but does not know the child's location, the first consideration of the social worker should be to locate the sibling. It's possible that the other child is in grave danger. The social worker may begin the search by trying to contact other family members, neighbors, or associates of the parents but may need the assistance of the police department.

55. B: Diagnostic *specifiers* in the *Diagnostic and Statistical Manual of Mental Disorders* (*DSM*), currently in its fifth edition, are used almost exclusively to indicate a diagnostic subtype or to rank the status or severity of a diagnostic condition. Many old specifiers and numerous new specifiers are now in use. Common specifiers include "generalized," "with mixed features," "with (or without) insight," "in controlled environment," "on maintenance therapy," "in partial remission," "in full remission," and "by prior history." Other specifiers are used to rank symptom severity (e.g., mild, moderate, and severe). While the NOS (not otherwise specified) acronym has been omitted, the NEC (not elsewhere classified) option has been continue or updated in some diagnostic categories, allowing for idiosyncratic presentations and/or early diagnostic ambiguity.

56. B: Although the criteria for a diagnosis of intellectual disability includes both cognitive capacity and adaptive functioning, the degree of severity (mild, moderate, severe or profound) is determined by adaptive functioning. Cognitive capacity is often measured by IQ scores. Intelligence quotient (IQ) scores include a margin for measurement error of five points. In the *DSM-5*, the term *Mental Retardation* has been replaced with *Intellectual Disability (intellectual developmental disorder)* or ID, to better conform to terms in medical and educational fields. While IQ scores have been removed from the diagnostic criteria, placing greater emphasis on *adaptive functioning*, testing is still necessary. Deficits must now exist in three domains: 1) intellectual functioning (e.g., reasoning, judgment, abstract thinking, and academic and experiential learning); 2) in personal independence and social responsibility (e.g., communication, self-care, home living, social/interpersonal skills, use of community resources, self-direction, functional academic skills, work, leisure, health, and safety); and 3) with onset during the "developmental period" (less rigid than "before age 18"). Supporting associated features include poor social judgment, gullibility, an inability to assess risk, etc.

57. D: *Language Disorder* is characterized by substantial impairment in speaking, as seen in lower scores on standardized tests of language use in the presence of otherwise normal cognitive capacity. Speech sound disorder (formerly called *Phonological Disorder)* presents as substantial impairment in making appropriate speech sounds, sufficient to impede success in academic, occupational, or interpersonal communication. Childhood-onset fluency disorder (*Stuttering*) involves a disturbance in the timing and fluency of speech, unrelated to age and normal development.

58. C: *Autism spectrum disorder* (ASD) presents with virtually all classic symptoms. Some with autism spectrum disorder tend to experience delays in language development and have below average IQ, while others tend to have an average or above average IQ and speak at their expected age range. Children with ASD often become obsessed with a single object or topic, and tend to talk about it nonstop. Social skills are significantly impaired, and they are frequently uncoordinated and awkward. ASD encompasses four disorders that previously under DSM-IV were separate, but are now all believed to be the same disease, with differing severity levels: autistic disorder (autism), Asperger's disorder, childhood disintegrative disorder, and pervasive developmental disorder. *Social communication disorder* cannot be diagnosed if the client presents with restricted repetitive behaviors. As most of these behaviors deal with social issues, and there is no mention of changed IQ, difficulty reasoning/thinking, or failures to be personally independent, *intellectual disability* would not be appropriate.

59. B: If a homeless client was a victim of assault and is being treated in the emergency room but refuses to file a complaint with the police even though the client recognized the perpetrator and he was the fourth homeless person to be attacked, the best response is: "Let the doctor treat you and then you can decide later about filing a complaint." The social worker should avoid trying to put undue pressure on the client but can discuss the reasons for filing a complaint after the client's immediate needs are attended to and may offer to accompany the client to file a complaint.

60. A: The most likely tentative diagnosis for this client is *pica*, which is characterized by the persistent ingestion of nonfood items and materials, demonstrated in her ingestion of paper, clay, and sand. Key features include compulsive craving for nonfood material (for some, ice; rarely, caused by mineral deficiency), and an otherwise normal use of normal foods. The classic symptoms of *Anorexia* center around a poor body image (e.g., seeing oneself as fat) and the avoidance of food to control weight. This may be accompanied by the use of laxatives and exercise to further manage body weight. *Bulimia nervosa* involves binging followed by purging (e.g., vomiting and/or laxative use). *Rumination disorder* involves regurgitating food and re-chewing it. In deriving a tentative diagnosis, note that this adolescent is not drastically losing weight, nor is she avoiding regular food, both which may indicate anorexia if such actions were present. There is no binge-purge cycle and no re-chewing of swallowed and regurgitated food which remove bulimia nervosa and rumination disorder as possible diagnoses.

61. D: *Encopresis* refers to incontinence of bowel in an individual who is at least 4 years of age, chronologically or mentally. It may occur due to stress, anxiety, or constipation, as oppositional or retaliatory behavior, and it may be either voluntary or involuntary. It must occur at least monthly for 3 consecutive months. It must not, however, be due to a neurological, medical, chemical-, or substance-induced disorder or stimulant. The term for similar problems with bladder incontinence is *enuresis*, which has similar diagnostic features, with the exception that bladder incontinence must occur at least twice a week over 3 consecutive months.

62. B: *Separation Anxiety Disorder* involves profound distress when an individual separated from the presence of a primary attachment figure. Onset must be before the age of 18, and the symptoms must be present for at least 4 weeks prior to diagnosis. Symptoms frequently include undue anxiety, irrational fears or worries about safety, inability to fall asleep alone, nightmares, and exaggerated homesickness. These symptoms may also be accompanied by somatic symptoms such as stomachache, dizziness, palpitations, or vomiting, which may lead to medical evaluation when the underlying disorder is psychological in nature. Symptoms during attachment figure separation are developmentally expected until a child reaches 3 to 5 years of age. Clinicians must first rule out agoraphobia before making this diagnosis, especially in older children. *Oppositional Defiant Disorder* requires rebelliousness; *Panic Disorder* involves intense generalized fear that something bad is about to happen; *Agoraphobia* (a type of Panic Disorder) involves severe anxiety in situations deemed uncomfortable, dangerous, or remote from help. None of these are relevant in this situation.

63. D: Both delirium (ICD-10 code of F05) and encephalopathy (G93.40), whether metabolic or toxic, are clinically virtually the same condition. Toxic encephalopathy/delirium occurs secondary to drugs (including alcohol), while metabolic refers to all other inducing mechanisms (sepsis, renal or hepatic failure, etc.). The term delirium tends to be used in psychiatry, while encephalopathy tends to be used in medicine, especially by neurologists. Of note, delirium is a nonspecific ICD (International Classification of Disease) code by Medicare (and thus, by most other payers). Some medical insurers will not reimburse for F05 (see ICD-10), as it falls into a "mental disorder" definition (within the ICD F code range). However, both terms refer to sudden-onset altered mental status conditions, most of which are reversible if the underlying cause is resolved. In elderly persons, medication toxicity and underlying infections with fever are typical causes of delirium/encephalopathy.

64. D: The best response is to advocate for the patient to be admitted for further medical evaluation. There is too much unknown about this seriously compromised elderly patient. He may be malnourished, toxic from overmedication, mildly septic without pyrexia (fever) or elevated WBC, particularly if a urinary tract infection is involved. Sending him back home, from where he apparently wandered away, would be unethical and inhumane. Placing him outside his home, even on a short-term basis, could further compromise his mental status and traumatize him. Delaying discharge until collateral contacts can be made is an option, but family cannot provide an adequate medical explanation for his condition and his safety is clearly at risk. Living alone and wandering suggests delirium (a sudden onset, likely reversible condition) rather than insidious dementia (slow onset, with irreversible impairment) With hospitalization, it can be seen if his condition clears or worsens, collateral contacts can be ensured, and underlying health problems can be explored and potentially resolved. Advocacy in such a situation is a key social work role.

65. B: If the social worker is interviewing a 48-year-old male and notes that the man has a prescription for clozapine, a psychotropic medicine, and other medications, the first action of the social worker should be to note the date on the bottles and count the numbers of pills remaining to try to determine if the man has likely been taking his medications. The social worker should gather as much information as possible before taking further action, such as contacting the man's physician or recommending a 72-hour psychiatric hold.

66. B: The client has at least two of the possible eleven criteria for alcohol use disorder. Most important are the ones that could change the course of his life (missing work and legal issues). Symptoms of withdrawal (delirium tremens, etc.) arise with the cessation of drinking but are not mentioned in this scenario, and may not occur as the client is said to just drink on the weekends. Symptoms of alcohol intoxication (slurred speech, impaired gait, attention and memory impairment, etc.) is not mentioned in this scenario. Recreational use involves sporadic ingestion at such times and in such a way as to avoid negative family, employment, and social consequences, but used heavily enough to produce a pleasurable (recreational) effect.

67. C: The client is clearly displaying both hallucinations (seeing things not there, objects floating) and delusions (believing things that are not true, thought control), as well as the rambling and disorganized speech characteristic of *Schizophrenia*. The condition has existed longer than 6 months, though it is currently in an acute phase. No subtype specifier is required, as the *DSM-5* no longer uses the prior specifiers (paranoid, disorganized, undifferentiated, etc.), with the exception of catatonic type. A diagnosis of *Bipolar Disorder* would not be correct, as there is no evidence of mood cycling and this is not an exacerbated manic phase with psychotic features. *Schizoaffective Disorder* would not be correct, as it requires the presence of a clear affective component (mania or depression), which is not in evidence either by history or presentation. *Substance-Induced Psychosis* requires the proximate use of a mind-altering substance (such as methamphetamine), which is also not in evidence. While there is a remote history (and one cannot entirely rule out more recent ingestion), the parents indicate the symptoms have been consistently present for the greater part of a year, which precludes the episodic presentation of Substance-Induced Psychosis.

68. D: The most appropriate early diagnosis would be Delusional Disorder, erotomanic type. The client openly indicates that this famous person has loving feelings for him, in spite of the fact they've never met or directly communicated in any way. Classic features of *erotomania* (sometimes also called de Clérambault syndrome) include identification with someone in higher status (famous, wealthy, etc.), and is more common among women than men. The symptoms are not infrequently manifest in either schizophrenia or bipolar mania, at which point either would be the proper primary diagnosis (e.g., bipolar, acute manic phase, with erotomanic features). *Grandiose type* is not correct as it focuses on a client's belief that he or she has special talents, unique understandings, or an unrecognized or unreported extraordinary accomplishment. *Jealous type* is not correct, as the inordinate jealousy must be centered in faulty perceptions of infidelity in a real relationship. *Persecutory type* is not correct, as it focuses on a fear of a conspiracy by others to do him harm.

69. B: The diagnosis of *Brief Psychotic Disorder* requires schizophrenic-like symptoms for at least 1 day and no longer than 1 month (e.g., such as hallucinations and/or delusions, both of which this client claimed). It cannot be due to drug-induced psychosis (illicit or licit drugs), or another medical condition. *Posttraumatic Stress Disorder* would not be appropriate as it is not characterized by schizophrenic-like symptoms, but rather flashbacks and trauma-linked stressors that are not indicated here. *Drug-induced psychosis* would not be appropriate, as the vignette specifically disclaims drug use. *Bipolar disorder* would not be correct, as there is no evidence of cycling (manic depression). Thus, Brief Psychotic Disorder is the diagnosis that best fits the available information.

70. C: To be diagnosed with cyclothymia, the moodiness must have been present for at least 2 years (at least 1 year in children and adolescents) and there must have been multiple periods with hypomanic symptoms that do not meet criteria for a manic episode and numerous periods with depressive symptoms that fall short of a major depressive episode. Additionally, the hypomanic and depressive periods must have been present at least half the time and never without the symptoms for more than 2 months at a time. Bipolar disorder involves more dramatic mood swings, with extreme mania and depression. Dysthymia is a form of depression that does not meet Major Depression criteria and does not have hypomanic or manic features. Mood Disorder NOS is not a DSM-5 disorder.

71. D: Persistent complex bereavement disorder is diagnosed when intense and compromising grief extends at least beyond the first year. Key features with the client is her sense of meaninglessness without her spouse, estrangement from others, emotional numbness, and preoccupying thoughts about dying to be with him again. The diagnosis of Major Depression would not be correct due to the fact that the focus is on the loss, rather than a generalized meaninglessness, hopelessness, and helplessness. Posttraumatic stress would not be correct because it centers on key features associated with experiencing an overwhelming and traumatic event (such as combat), with flashbacks and other emotions tied directly to the event itself, rather than to a loss. Uncomplicated bereavement would not be correct, as the intensity and compromising features of the loss are not resolving over time, but rather becoming overly protracted. Of note, *DSM-5* has removed the "bereavement exclusion." It is possible to be diagnosed both with bereavement and major depression, if the circumstances warrant.

72. A: Bipolar I involves mania and Bipolar II involves primarily depression. Bipolar I Disorder requires a minimum of one manic episode (or mixed episode), as well as episodes with features typical of Major Depression. In contrast to this, Bipolar II requires at least one Major Depression episode, and a minimum of at least one Hypomanic episode. Adequate control requires medications. Preferred treatment medications more commonly focus on atypical antipsychotics (Abilify, Geodon, Risperdal, Seroquel, or Zyprexa), which provide greater symptom relief than the older mood stabilizing medications such as lithium, Depakote, or Tegretol. These are now more commonly used only as adjuncts. An extended depressive episode may also be treated with antidepressants. Education about the condition, as well as therapy (e.g., cognitive-behavior, interpersonal, social rhythm, family therapy), greatly enhances successful management.

73. D: These symptoms most closely resemble panic disorder. The symptoms of a panic attack appear very quickly and generally peak within 10 minutes. Typical symptoms include rapid heart rate, shortness of breath, light-headedness, trembling, derealization and depersonalization (feeling surreal and detached from self), nausea, dizziness, numb and tingling feelings, etc. These are typically accompanied by feelings of impending doom and/or death. Many of the symptoms are a direct result of hyperventilation during the acute panic phase. Anxiety disorder due to a medical condition is not correct, as there is no underlying medical condition. Generalized anxiety disorder is not correct, as it does not have sudden onset but rather is an accumulation of worry and anxiety that persists for 6 or more months (without an underlying medical condition or substance use precipitant). Acute stress disorder is not correct, as it involves a precipitating PTSD-like traumatic event that induces the symptoms of stress.

74. C: The key features of Illness Anxiety Disorder (care-seeking type) include an intense preoccupation with the acquisition of a serious health problem, an absence of actual somatic symptoms (or only very mild symptoms), an honest belief and fear of an illness (e.g., not manipulative in any way), a high level of health anxiety, and excessive health-preoccupied behaviors that have continued for more than 6 months. Care-seeking type can be specified, as the client continues to seek help and support from a medical provider on a regular basis, even after adequate reassurances have been provided. Malingering Disorder is not correct, as it involves exaggerating or falsely claiming symptoms for secondary gain (e.g., insurance claims, to be relieved of unpleasant work). Factitious Disorder is not correct, as it involves the deliberate fabrication of symptoms without the intent to receive tangible or concrete rewards, but rather for the nurturance or attention thereby derived. Somatic Symptom Disorder is not correct, as it requires the presence of actual somatic (physical) symptoms. Note: Somatization Disorder, Hypochondriasis, Pain Disorder, and Undifferentiated Somatoform Disorder have been removed from *DSM-5* and replaced with Somatic Symptom Disorder.

75. B: Key features of dissociative amnesia with dissociative fugue are localized or selective amnesia surrounding certain events, or generalized amnesia involving identity and life history, along with some sort of purposeful travel or simply aimless wandering. The amnesia must produce significant distress, and/or impairment in social, occupational, or other significant areas of personal function. It must not be a result of substance ingestion or a medical (especially neurological) condition. Dissociative Identity Disorder (in the past known as Multiple Personality Disorder) would not be correct as it involves the development to one or more separate identities.

76. B: Genito-pelvic pain disorder refers to any form of pain during sexual intercourse that persistently recurs. Causes can include involuntary contractions of the outer third of the vagina (involving the pubococcygeus muscles), vaginal dryness, inflammation, infection, skin conditions, sexually transmitted infections (STIs), or any other underlying medical condition. Female sexual interest/arousal disorder would not be correct because it involves a psychological aversion to or avoidance of sexual activity, rather than physical pain. Female Orgasmic Disorder is incorrect because it involves a failure to reach orgasm, even with appropriate stimulation, excluding an underlying medical condition.

77. D: The most likely diagnosis to describe this behavior would be other specified paraphilia. Exhibitionism involves a minimum of 6 months of recurrent urges, fantasies, and/or behaviors involving the exposure of one's genitals to an unsuspecting person, or where clinically significant distress or impairment in social, occupational, or other meaningful areas of functioning occurs. In this case, however, the recipient of the client's disrobing behaviors is not an unsuspecting stranger, nor does the vignette specify that she exposes her genitals or if she fully or only partially disrobes. Thus, this is more an act of consensual sex-play, rather than exhibitionism. Voyeurism is not correct, as it involves watching an unsuspecting person disrobing. Frotteurism is inaccurate as it involves intense sexual arousal from the urge, fantasy, or act of touching or rubbing against a nonconsenting person.

78. B: If a 15-year-old client persists in making suggestive remarks about the social worker's appearance and asks if the social worker is married or has a partner, the most appropriate response is one that not only clearly sets limits but also gives the reason: "It's not appropriate for us to discuss personal information, and I feel uncomfortable with your comments." The social worker should focus on "I" rather than "you" and should speak clearly and directly but avoid any indications of anger.

79. C: Borderline Personality Disorder is characterized by, among other features, a pervasive pattern of unstable relationships, chronic feelings of emptiness, poorly controlled chronic anger, and alternating devaluing and overvaluing relationships, followed by frantic efforts to avoid abandonment. Histrionic Personality Disorder would not be appropriate, as the client's high emotions and attention-seeking behaviors are just a subset of other problematic issues, beliefs, and behaviors. Narcissistic Personality Disorder is also not correct, as the client's problems are not centered on grandiosity, absence of empathy, arrogance, or entitlement, etc. Antisocial Personality Disorder would be incorrect, as features of aggression, violations of the law, or absence of remorse are not central to the client's presentation. The presence of a personality disorder, however, is clear, as the issues involve a pattern of interacting with the world that guides her life and shapes her experiences.

80. D: All of the listed terms are all used interchangeably. Common guidelines for direct practice include: 1) Start with client-identified issues. 2) Use positive goal setting. 3) Overcome difficulties by modeling honest and direct communication. 4) Ensure culturally competent service by careful assessment. 5) Use a client's native language, if possible, or obtain an interpreter. 6) Avoid reality testing a delusional client's thoughts, and instead seek to calm and support pending further assessment and/or medications. 7) Carefully watch for transference and countertransference processes. If a client requires hospitalization, seek a voluntary placement where possible, and carefully follow involuntary hospitalization and evaluation guidelines when necessary.

81. A: If the social worker is utilizing role playing in group therapy and the client has enacted his role in a problem situation with a partner and then the social workers suggests they practice mirroring, this would involve the partner reflecting the behavior displayed by the client. Thus, if the client paces back and forth and frowns, the partner would also pace and frown. The purpose of mirroring is to allow the client to see how his behavior is observed and perceived by others.

82. B: While life transitions can be stressful, these transitions tend to be gradual and thus lack the short-term and overwhelming qualities that properly define a crisis. Cultural-Societal crises are those where fundamental worldviews collide in traumatic ways, for example, immigrating to a foreign country, or revealing homosexuality in a heterosexual community. Maturational crises involve developmental events, such as beginning school, leaving home, or marriage. Situational crises involve a sudden traumatic event, such as a car accident, witnessing violence, or being assaulted. To help individuals re-establish their coping skills and equilibrium, Crisis Intervention has three primary goals: 1) reducing the impact and symptoms that accompany a crisis (e.g., normalizing, calming, empowering); 2) mobilizing resources, both internal (psychological) and external (e.g., social, financial); and 3) restoring the precrisis level of function.

83. D: If the social worker's client has few resources and many issues and the social worker is utilizing the principle of partialization, the first actions should be to collaborate with the client in creating a list of problems and them to group them and identify the highest priority. The principle of partialization aims to help manage complex situations by focusing on one problem at a time and setting priorities with initial focus on the problem that is most critical.

84. D: The Premack Principle is a method for increasing desired behaviors. The *Premack Principle* is applied by pairing a low-probability behavior with a high-probability behavior in order to increase the frequency that the low-probability behavior will be engaged. For example, a child will be permitted to play sports, watch television, or play video games only after he or she has completed all daily assigned homework. In this way, the motivation and desire to complete assigned homework is increased. This is a form of *Operant Conditioning*. Other Operant Conditioning tools include: 1) The use of *Reinforcers* (positive consequences following a desired behavior). Reinforcers may be *primary* (naturally reinforcing, such as needs for food, water, and sleep), or *secondary* (a stimulus that an organism learns to value). *Positive reinforcement* involves a stimulus reward following a desired behavior, and *negative reinforcement* involves the withdrawal of an unpleasant consequence when desired behavior occurs.

85. D: A *Contingency Contract* is used in treatment to specify a particular consequence, either positive or negative, contingent upon whether or not a specific behavior or behaviors occur as agreed upon. It is a meaningful tool for modifying individual behavior. Another commonly used *Operant Conditioning* tool to reinforce desirable behavior is called the *Token Economy*. It involves the delivery of representative tokens that can be redeemed for desirable reinforcers by the individual. It is most commonly used with children to modify behavior. Other concurrently used strategies include the use of *verbal prompts* and *clarifications*. As reminders (prompts) are provided and clarifications are supplied to increase understanding and focus, behaviors can be more rapidly modified and solidified.

86. A: Three forms of cognitive-behavioral therapy (CBT) predominate: 1) Aaron Beck's *Cognitive Therapy* views depression and mental illness as a bias toward negative thinking via thinking errors (all-or-nothing and black-and-white/dichotomous thinking, emotional reasoning, overgeneralization, magnification and minimization, catastrophizing, and mind reading). Relief is found through collaborative empiricism, Socratic dialogue, guided discovery, decatastrophizing, reattribution training, and decentering. 2) Albert Ellis' *Rational Emotive Therapy* identifies common irrational beliefs (demands and absolutes), which are rationally challenged, evaluated, clarified, and resolved. 3) Donald Meichenbaum's *Self-Instruction Training* focuses on maladaptive self-statements that frequently underlie negative thinking patterns, negativity, and self-defeating thoughts and behaviors. Therapy involves thought assessments, situational self-statement exploration, and developing new self-statements that better reflect truth and mental health.

87. C: The key components of *Solution-Focused Therapy* include the following: 1) problem description; 2) formulating goals; 3) collaboratively identifying solutions; 4) feedback at close of session; and 5) evaluation of progress. *Dialectical Behavioral Therapy* is most often used in the treatment of Borderline Personality Disorder, and consists of four modules: 1) mindfulness (observe, describe, and then participate); 2) interpersonal effectiveness (learning to assertively ask for change and say no when needed); 3) distress tolerance (identifying and tolerating things that cannot be changed); and 4) emotion regulation (becoming emotionally aware and able to direct emotions). *Reality Therapy* focuses on meeting four psychological needs (belonging, freedom, fun, and power) through internally oriented, purposeful behaviors. It rejects the medical model of mental illness, and side-steps past attitudes, behaviors, and feelings in favor of current perspectives on whether any given behavior can responsibly meet one's needs without damaging others. Reality testing is used to reject unsuccessful behaviors and identify those that will truly succeed.

88. B: Karen Horney concurred with Freud that anxiety underlies most neuroses. However, she disagreed that conflicts between instinctual drives and the superego produced this anxiety. Rather, anxiety arises through problematic parental behaviors: rejection, over-protectiveness, and/or indifference. Children cope by: 1) over-compliance (moving toward people), 2) detachment (moving away from people), or 3) aggression (moving against people). Resolution requires: 1) meeting biological needs, and 2) protection from danger, fear, and pain. *Erich Fromm* also moved past Freud and Marx, believing that individuals can transcend biological and societal barriers through pursuit of internal freedom. Efforts to escape freedom (responsibility) produce self-alienation and "unproductive" families that favor symbiosis (enmeshment) or withdrawal (indifference). He identified four problematic personality orientations: 1) receptive, 2) exploitative, 3) hoarding, and 4) marketing, and one healthy orientation, 5) productive (rational responsibility). Harry Stack Sullivan emphasized relationships over lifespan issues, focusing on three modes of cognitive experience in personality development: 1) Prototaxic (momentary perceptions in early life); 2) Parataxic (misperceptions or distortions of early important events); and 3) Syntaxic (the emergence of logical, sequential, modifiable, and internally consistent thinking).

89. D: Carl Jung developed the concept of *abreaction*, which involves relieving, retelling, and reorienting an experience to discharge the negative psychological burdens that accompany the experience. Abreaction is a form of *catharsis*, where abreaction involves dealing with specific biographical experiences and catharsis involves the release of more generalized emotional and physical tension. Jung felt that behavior is derived from past experiences in the context of future goals and aspirations. Personality is two-fold: the *conscious*, oriented toward the external world, and the *unconscious*. The unconscious is composed of personal and collective elements. *Personal unconscious* consists of repressed or forgotten experiences, and the *collective unconscious* consists of inherited memory traces and primordial images (*archetypes*) that produce commonly shared understandings in societies. Key archetypes include the *self* (producing unity in the personality), the *persona* (a public mask), the *shadow* (or dark side) of personality, and the *anima* (feminine) or *animus* (masculine). Personality consists of attitudes (introversion and extroversion) and four basic functions (feeling, intuiting, sensing, and thinking).

90. D: Introjection refers to gradually defining oneself by thoughtful rejection or integration of outside ideas. Gestalt Therapy differs from Freudian Psychoanalysis on introjection primarily in its definition of a gradual rather than immediate construct. Psychoanalysis posits a prompt and full acceptance by the client of the analyst's conclusions, whereas Gestalt suggests a gradual integration of only that information that the client deems accurate following due reflection. Four key boundary disturbances defined in Gestalt Therapy are: 1) introjection: differentiating between "me, and not me," lacking which a client is overly compliant and attempts to please others at the loss of true self; 2) projection: assigning uncomfortable aspects of the self to others (e.g., "he never liked me," when it is you who dislikes him); 3) retroflection: directing inward the feelings one has for another (seen as expressions of self-blame when addressing such feelings with another); and 4) confluence: an absence of boundaries between self and others, resulting in feelings of both guilt and resentment over actual differences. The therapeutic goal is to create healthy boundaries and self-integration (integrity).

91. D: This groups is best described as an ongoing growth group. Generally, groups are defined as either task or treatment oriented. Open-ended groups have no termination date. Task groups are formed solely to accomplish a specific goal (preparing a New Year's dance, etc.). Treatment groups serve to enhance members' social and/or emotional needs and/or skills. Types of treatment groups include: 1) educational groups: formed to enhance learning about specific issues or problems, providing needed information and skills; 2) growth groups: focus on personal enrichment and progress, as opposed to remediating past problems and concerns; 3) socialization groups: aid members in accommodating role and environmental challenges (e.g., a new immigrants group); 4) support groups: bring together people with common issues or circumstances to help them in coping with their shared concerns (e.g., a bereavement group); and 5) therapy groups: serve to offer remediation and/or rehabilitation of a specific concern or problem (e.g., a gambling problem group).

92. C: If the social worker is working on a project with a coworker who persists in berating the social worker for missing a meeting scheduled when the social worker had to deal with a client emergency and must ask for information but realizes this will give the coworker another opportunity to complain, the most effective assertive communication is: "I realize I missed the meeting and that was inconvenient for you, but what did the data show?" This response begins with an "I" statement and defuses the possible complaints by stating them upfront and then asks directly for information needed.

93. B: Triangulation is the introduction of a third party into a conflict between two individuals. The goal is to produce a power asymmetry in order to turn events to one's favor. Family problems typically involve triangulation. Therapeutic triangulation occurs when a social worker is drawn into taking sides. The eight interlocking concepts of Family Systems Theory include: 1) *Self-Differentiation* (vs. fused identities); 2) *Nuclear Family Emotional System* (formerly the *Undifferentiated Family Ego Mass*) of fused identity; 3) *Triangles* (drawing a third party into conflicts); 4) *Societal Emotional Process* (emotional processes in societal interactions, similar to family); 5) *Emotional Cutoff* (severing intergenerational ties); 6) *Sibling Position* (drives some personality characteristics); 7) *Family Projection Process* (parents transmitting patterns to offspring); and 8) *Multigenerational Transmission Process* (patterns transmitted intergenerationally).

94. C: Equifinality refers to the idea that the same results can be secured in different ways. The *Circular Model of Causality*, however, notes that the behaviors of different subsystems can nevertheless reciprocally influence each other. Responses B and D are not formal Communications/Experimental Therapy terms. Other forms of dysfunctional communication include criticizing, blaming, mind-reading, implying events that can be modified or improved are unalterable, overgeneralizations, double-bind expressions (contradictory demands that functionally allow only one of two required consequences to be achieved), denying that one is communicating (which can never be true), and disqualifying other's communications.

95. A: If a 4-year-old child has been placed into foster care for the second time because his mother was charged with child endangerment after leaving the child unattended while she engaged in prostitution, the first goal for permanency planning should be family reunification with the mother. While the child appears healthy and well cared for, the child must also be safe, so the social worker must work with the parent to develop plans for childcare. Being a sex-worker does not preclude a person from being a good parent.

96. A: The concept of *complementarity* addresses the harmony and disharmony that arises when family roles cannot be reconciled. *Alignments* are coalitions that are produced between various family subsystems to achieve specific goals, the nature of which may or may not be dysfunctional. *Power hierarchies* reveal the distribution of power within the family as a whole. *Disengagement* occurs when family members and subsystems become emotionally and/or interactively isolated. Of further note: *subsystems* are separate functional family units (e.g., parents) that operate within the larger family structure. *Enmeshment* results from over-involvement or concern with family members to the point that individual recognition and autonomy are lost. *Inflexibility* addresses situations in which the family structure becomes so rigid that adaptation cannot occur when required.

97. D: *Circular questions* are used to enhance relational perspectives by helping family members to take the standpoint of another, particularly with a family member who may otherwise be misunderstood. *Hypothesizing* is something done by the therapy team, wherein they attempt to understand the presenting problem and formulate a successful intervention, refining throughout the therapeutic process. *Counter-paradox* is an extension of *paradoxical prescription* (wherein problem behaviors are actually prescribed) by which a problem behavior and all related interactions around it are prescribed. *Positive connotation* reframes problematic symptoms as efforts to preserve the family and promote solidarity. Other techniques include *neutrality* (in which social worker-family member alliances are avoided to prevent triangulation}, and *rituals* (repetitive behaviors used to counter dysfunctional family rules).

98. C: The community itself. Community organization involves work with larger entities, citizen groups, and organization directors for the purpose of: 1) solving social problems; 2) developing collaborative and proactive qualities in community members; and 3) redistributing decision-making power through community relationships. Community organizers assist communities to learn how to meet their needs, eradicate social problems, and enrich lives, as well as balancing resources and social welfare needs. To accomplish this, the community must first be accepted as it is, and then learn of the interdependence of its constituent members and intra-community entities.

99. B: Social workers often serve as community organizers, and may readily be approached with problems in the community. In this situation, the first and best step for the citizen to take is as a whistleblower. This step draws attention to the problem, activates oversight agencies, and begins to bring a problem out into the open. Next steps may include: 2) negotiation with the factory leadership; 3) community education, to help others understand the problem; 4) social protesting (picketing, demonstrations, boycotting); 5) lobbying entities responsible to intervene; 6) conducting action research to further explore the problems; 7) forming self-help groups to assist the oppressed to better understand resources and their rights; and 8) legal efforts such as mediation and/or lawsuits to compel change.

100. B: Only an attorney can offer legal counsel and advice. A social worker can, however, point out options and refer a client or community to appropriate resources for legal counsel and advice. Other intervention roles that may be assumed by a social worker include: 1) broker: identifying and referring clients to needed resources within a community; 2) case manager: assisting clients lacking the capacity to take independent action and/or follow through with resource referrals; 3) client advocate: working on behalf or in conjunction with clients seeking access to needed resources; and 4) mediator: collaborating with both the client and resource provider(s) to overcome conflicts and obstacles in identifying a path to receive needed services and resources.

101. C: Involuntary clients may utilize humor in their interactions, but not as a primary mechanism for resisting the treatment process. More commonly, resistance comes in the forms of: 1) aggression: becoming either verbally or even physically assaultive, or producing a pseudo-cooperative passive-aggressive response that needs to be mitigated before meaningful progress can be made; 2) diversion: commonly seen through blaming ("someone else made this happen"), seeking to turn attention to others ("he did something way worse"), shifting the focus back to the social worker ("you think you're better than the rest of us"), or simply guiding the discussion in another direction; and 3) withdrawal: seen as a refusal to talk, avoiding discussions about feelings, or minimizing relevant issues, etc. Each of these forms of resistance must be overcome before treatment can properly proceed.

102. B: The primary objective of supervision is meeting the clients' individual needs. It is important to recognize the difference in purpose between supervision and supervising tasks. The primary purpose of supervision is to ensure that clients' needs are fully, ethically, and competently addressed and met. To accomplish this, the supervisor must also ensure that staff have adequate training and necessary access to resources and services. The supervisor must also establish and conduct quality control reviews to regularly monitor the work of agency staff and outside providers. The primary task of the supervisor is to ensure that essential work is completed. This is necessary to keep the agency functioning and to ensure that an appropriate number of clients can be served. This requires both administrative and clinical expertise on the part of the supervisor and his or her designated leaders within the agency.

103. A: The purpose of consultation is to share expertise, seek options, consider recommendations, and otherwise collaborate and explore clinical and/or operational needs and resources and optimal options. Consultation is not designed to serve as alternate leadership, to be directive or determinative, or to serve as a deferral opportunity such that leaders or staff relinquish their obligation to continue to carry out their professional responsibilities. Consultation may be considered in six stages: 1) entry (early contracting, orientation, and overcoming resistance; 2) identifying consultation goals (which requires adequate problem exploration and understanding); 3) defining goals (which must be a collaborative venture); 4) providing intervention(s) (supported by brainstorming and Delphi methods to obtain participation from all); 5) assessment (of progress and continuing or new problems); 6) concluding the relationship (involves fostering independence, determining continuing availability, etc.).

104. D: The structuralist management style views organizations as deeply impacted by environmental factors, with conflict as inevitable but not necessarily negative if handled properly. Bureaucratic theories (Max Weber) espouse vertical hierarchy, policy-driven, merit rewards, and a careful division of labor that maximizes efficiency and control. Scientific theories utilize an economic and rational perspective to maximize productivity. Contingency theories focus on flexibility and responsiveness. Participative theories conclude that democratic leadership and participant buy-in make for greater loyalty and productivity. Quality Circles are based on self-governance and evaluation. Total Quality Management (TQM) focuses on service delivery processes and a broader view than Quality Assurance models. Maslow's Hierarchy of Needs theory allows management to ensure greater participant fulfillment and thus job satisfaction and productivity. Job Enrichment theory (Herzberg) posits that good job "hygiene" (benefits, conditions, salary, etc.) plus motivators (freedom, challenges, growth, etc.) optimized management outcomes. Needs Theory (McClelland) views the paramount needs as power, affiliation, and achievement as the path to optimal management and staff success.

105. C: *Summative Program Evaluation* examines the degree to which goals and objectives are realized, as well as how generalizable the outcomes may be to other settings and populations, in determining program efficacy and value. *Cost-Benefit Analysis* produces a ratio of direct costs to outcome benefits in determining program effectiveness. *Cost Effectiveness* evaluation focuses on a program's operational costs as compared with final output (unit) costs, requiring a favorable ratio to deem a program effective. *Formative Program Evaluation* is conducted longitudinally (from program inception through implementation) to determine its final efficacy and value. *Peer Review* involves collegial evaluations using professional standards to determine the quality of work and the resultant outcomes.

106. C: If a client is being treated for anxiety but reports having difficulty concentrating on schoolwork and tasks because of being unable to stop worrying and has been sleeping poorly and has lost weight, the complementary therapeutic approach that the social worker should advise first is relaxation exercises, such as deep breathing and visual imagery. These exercises are easy to teach and to learn and can be mastered very quickly, so the client can utilize the exercises immediately.

107. B: A given state's Division of Child and Family Services (DCFS, though sometimes called by other titles in various states) would not typically provide safe shelters for victims of domestic violence. They would, however, provide referrals and linkages for services of this nature to ensure the safety of individuals who are in an unsafe home environment. Services commonly provided directly include therapy services, educational referrals, employment training, family counseling and intervention, and other services designed to mitigate family problems and restore successful family functioning. Within most DCFS programs are Child Protective Services (CPS) programs that offer services such as investigations of abuse, shelter care, family therapy, juvenile court linkages, foster care, and other services and resources to help stabilize difficult home situations.

108. D: The first step should be to promptly refer the asthmatic boy to a medical doctor. Asthma can be life-threatening, and the child is also described as congested and unwell. Given that "all" possessions were lost, it is reasonable to conclude that the child has little or no remaining inhaler medicines for an asthma crisis. While all may attend the medical visit, the boy needs to be seen urgently. Following or concurrently, a complete psychosocial evaluation needs to be completed. After further evaluation, the key elements of a case presentation for the director should include: 1) psychosocial history: mental health issues and social history such as living situation, finances, education, etc.; 2) individual issues: substance abuse history, legal history, physical abuse and neglect history, as well as resources, strengths, and resiliency, etc.; 3) family history, family dynamics, and extended family resources; 4) potential community resources and supports; 5) diversity issues: culture, language, race/ethnicity, orientation, etc.; 6) potential ethical issues and presenting issues in self-determination; and 7) intervention recommendations, including requisite resources.

109. C: SOAP stands for Subjective, Objective, Assessment, Plan. This method of documentation or charting is frequently used by health care providers to structure their clinical notes. An entry typically includes some or all of the following information: 1) Subjective information: information reported by the client and others closely involved. 2) Objective information: such as laboratory results, test scores, examination data, and scores from screenings. 3) Assessment: the summary review and ultimate conclusions derived from the subjective reports and objective tests, evaluations, examinations, screenings, etc., concluding in an overall impression of the presenting problem(s). 4) Plan: the steps that need to be taken to resolve the presenting problem(s), as derived from all prior information and conclusions drawn.

110: D. Social functioning is the service delivery model used by the social worker who focuses on helping the client to deal with current behavior in social interactions with a goal of the client's exhibiting behavior that is more acceptable to others. This often results in positive reinforcement, further encouraging socially behavior modification. The social functioning model is concerned less with issues that arose in the past and more with those in the present.

111. C: If the social worker in on the committee to update the policy and procedure manual, the social worker should recognize the first step in developing policies is to identify problems. Each problem should be assessed to determine how it has arisen, the conditions under which it is evident, and the stakeholders involved in or affected by the problem. Next, issues related to the problem, such as whether it is localized or generalized, should be identified and potential solutions brainstormed and then rank-ordered in order to choose the most appropriate solution from which to develop the policy.

112. C: If the social worker is in charge of an outreach program that is its own cost center and the organization utilizes a zero-based approach to departmental budgets and the budget period is coming to an end, the most appropriate action for the social worker is to prepare a report on the benefits of the program and the projected budget needs. With zero-based budgets, all cost centers are re-evaluated each budget period to determine if they should be funded or eliminated, partially or completely.

113. C: Social work ethics may best be defined as conduct standards based on values. A belief system is defined by core values, and ethics operationalize the values-defined belief system into standard of conduct. The core values of the social work profession are as follows (NASW, 2008): 1) dignity and worth of the individual; 2) the importance of human relationships; 3) the pursuit of social justice; 4) competence in professional knowledge and practice; 5) personal and professional integrity; and 6) service. The NASW Code of Social Work Ethics applies to all who practice social work, whether or not they belong to the NASW. There are six ethical areas: 1) responsibilities to clients; 2) responsibilities to colleagues; 3) responsibilities in practice settings; 4) responsibilities as professionals; 5) responsibilities to the profession; and 6) responsibilities to society.

114. D: Self-determination refers to the right to personal autonomy and decision making. Social workers are charged with helping their clients choose their own life's direction and destiny. An exception is when a client's choices are suicidal, homicidal, or abusive of others' rights. True self-determination requires: 1) the internal capacity for autonomy, 2) freedom from external constraints, and 3) information to make well-informed choices. Social workers should primarily assist clients in identifying and clarifying their own goals, rather than goals others might choose for them. Involuntary hospitalization or other mandated limits placed on self-determination do not allow professionals to fully ignore this ethical principle. Thus, the concepts of "least restrictive" and "least intrusive" come into play. Involuntary or mandated courses of action should be used only as a last result as is possible, without unduly risking the client's life or intruding upon or abusing other individuals.

115. A: The lack of signage on a substance abuse treatment facility is not an element of confidentiality. *Confidentiality* refers to an individual's right to control how identifiable information the client has divulged, or data about that individual, is handled, managed, and disseminated. Through confidentiality, individuals can retain control over the circumstances, timing, and extent to which personally sensitive information is shared with others. *Privacy* does not relate to information or data, but rather to the person themselves. Thus, privacy involves control over the circumstances, timing, and extent to which one wishes to share oneself physically, intellectually, and/or behaviorally with others. It is practiced by interviews in closed areas (not for information or data reasons, but for allowing expressions of emotion, sharing of thought processes, etc.), proper changing areas, and excusing others (including family, at times) from sharing experiences, etc. Confidentiality and privacy may be compromised for serious safety concerns, for the client or others.

116. C: The best response is to consult with a supervisor or legal counsel to ensure a proper response to the situation. It is significant to note that the NASW Code of Ethics (2008), Standard 1.09, bans all sexual involvement with both current and former clients and offers no time or circumstances limitation. Violation of this standard will thus result in prompt termination of any NASW membership. It is also important to note, however, that state licensing statutes vary on the topic (e.g., some states do not prohibit former client relationships at all, or may cite a 1 to 2 year prohibition only, after which such relationships are possible) and confidentiality requirements in such situations may also be complex; indeed, reporting may circumvent confidentiality in many ways. Therefore, it is important to know relevant state laws, and to seek competent consultation from a skilled supervisor or legal advisor.

117. D: The most appropriate response is to allow only a partial review, withholding portions deemed too sensitive. Clients have the right to reasonable access to records kept about them personally. However, social workers also have an obligation to prevent a client from reading case notes deemed potentially harmful to the client, or that could breach confidentiality of others (e.g., a party reporting suspected abuse). In situations where appropriate explanations would suffice to mitigate any concern of harm, the social worker has the right to review the case record with the client to offer explanatory insights and understandings. Where harm cannot be otherwise avoided, the social worker must restrict the client from viewing any harmful portion. For such portions, summary notes can be produced for the client, if desired. Regardless, it should be noted in the file the date and time of the client's review, and the rationale for any restrictions on review should be fully explained and documented in the case record.

118. A: The best response is to refer the child to a social worker with experience in pediatric sleep disorders. Obtaining licensure is only a first step in establishing a competent clinical practice. Remaining in areas of clear clinical expertise is ethically important, and not leading families to believe that one possesses skills that have not yet been developed is essential. When a new issue arises that is very closely related a social worker's primary scope of practice, it is reasonable to broaden skills through collateral research and consultation. However, if a treatment area (e.g., pediatric sleep disorders) is entirely beyond the scope of practice, it would be inappropriate to try to produce requisite skills through brief reading or consultation, when the skills actually require extended training and experience to develop. In such situations it is essential that the client be referred to another clinician for proper evaluation of the presenting problem.

119. D: If the social worker works in a program for homeless youth and is interested in engaging in fundraising to provide an increased budget for the program, the first step should be to define the purpose of the fundraising so that potential donors have a very clear understanding. Then, the goal for fundraising should be established and should be realistic because further support is more likely if the initial goal is reached. The social worker must also establish a budget for fundraising as there are almost always costs involved. Last, the target population must be determined as this will influence the fundraising approach.

120. C: The best way to secure the consult is to set up a formal consultation appointment to discuss the issue(s) in the office. It is tempting to discuss client cases over a meal or after hours, as it saves work time and allows for more informal sharing. However, discussing clients in a public setting produces a substantial likelihood that client confidentiality will be breached with others seated or walking nearby. It may also seem easier to leave a client's file with a consultant for review, as the consultant can then thoroughly review the case and more closely examine all specifically relevant issues. However, it is unethical for a primary social worker to disclose more client information to a consultant than is essential for the consulting issue to be properly addressed. Leaving a client file with the consultant offers no confidentiality boundaries at all. Consequently, consultation in an office setting, during a formal appointment, and by direct confidentiality-focused dialogue is the proper way to obtain an ethically structured consultation.

121. C: The first responsibility of the social worker is to contact the colleague and discuss treatment options. As with any client, the most appropriate intervention is one that occurs voluntarily and openly, with adequate support and caring concern offered. If the colleague refuses to seek immediate help in this situation, then further steps are necessary, including reporting the problem to a supervisor who can the address the issue further in accordance with agency policy and guidelines. Certainly the safety and well-being of the colleague's clients must be preserved, and no delay in addressing the issue can be afforded. Similar guidelines apply to colleagues who unethically practice outside the scope of their area of competence, or who behave unethically with clients, coworkers, or other outside programs and staff.

122. B: The best response is to seek to bring the agency's policies and procedures into compliance. Simply quitting does nothing to resolve this underlying problem with ethics and standards of conduct. Neither does a blanket refusal to work with materials, resources, and conditions that are outside NASW Code of Ethics standards. Optimally, a social worker should utilize his or her professional skills to seek to bring about change. Explaining the applicable ethical standards, and pointing out the protections they afford both staff and clients, provides a compelling case for change. If no progress is subsequently made, it may become necessary for the social worker to resign and leave the work setting, and/or to report the ethical issues to any proper oversight entity. In this way, ethical standards can be provided to all clients in any agency setting.

123. D: If the shared governance model used by the organization allows each department autonomous decision-making regarding issues that directly apply to that department, the leader of each department is a member of the administrative council, and the social worker is interested in make a major change in procedure that involves multiple departments, the social worker should first discuss the proposal with members of the different departments to build consensus.

124. A: If the social worker has been working with homeless clients for many months and has developed compassion fatigue from encountering the same problems over and over again, the social worker is likely to respond to clients with numbness toward their suffering and may begin to blame them for their problems rather than feeling empathy toward them. The social worker may need to take a break or rotate assignments in order to gain some perspective. Otherwise, other departments may feel that the social work department is imposing changes to which they have had no input.

125. B: Empathy is the most important feature of a meaningful therapeutic bond. Compassion involves concern for the misfortunes and welfare of another. Condolence involves expressions of compassion and sympathy. Sympathy literally means to feel with, or have a resonate feeling for another. Feelings of compassion and sympathy are expressed in carefully chosen words of condolence. *Empathy*, however, is deeper. It literally means to "feel into" the heart and mind of another, projecting oneself into their situation, feelings, and experiences. The term originated in psychology, drawn as a translation from a German term. It is an important tool in creating a therapeutic bond, as it involves a shared emotional state most fully realized when one has "been there," whereas sympathy is the natural state when one has not. Other important components of a strong therapeutic relationship include: 1) *warmth* (a show of genuine care and acceptance); 2) *authenticity/genuineness* (open and natural sharing in a meaningful way); and 3) *trust* (which involves a certainty of safety and predictability, and is maintained by practices such as confidentiality and privacy).

126. D: It can become easy to use short-hand descriptors to refer to one's caseload. However, doing so can subtly but powerfully alter the way a case manager feels and even interacts with clients. Far better to describe a caseload as "numerous people with schizophrenia, several people with bipolar disorder, and some other clients struggling with borderline personality disorder." The use of the words *people* and *clients* lets them retain their humanity. Everyone needs to be seen as an individual with unique qualities and contributions. Casually categorizing and stereotyping clients can lead to losing sight of their humanity, individuality, and uniqueness. Casework is and must remain client-focused, respectful, and understanding of clients' unique circumstances, needs, and potential. Using care in the verbiage chosen to speak about clients can help social work case managers avoid the biases, prejudices, and cultural insensitivities that can otherwise enter the case management process.

127. A: Allowing judgment of how acceptable or not the feelings are is not going to aid in the process of sharing. Feelings should not be appraised judgmentally. Rather, they should be evaluated for how they are affecting the client and how functional they are in the processes of living and interacting with others. Expressions of feelings offer an important window into understanding how a client perceives his or her life situation, as well as their sense of hopefulness, security, and safety. If feelings and emotions become too negative and burdensome, it may become important to incorporate the management of the client's feelings into the ongoing evaluation and treatment plan. Finally, if received and handled well, the sharing of deep feelings in a long-term case management or treatment processes further strengthens the therapeutic bond, which in turn enhances the effectiveness of the case manager/social worker in addressing the client's challenges and problems.

128. D: The best response is to seek to understand his feelings while soothing/deescalating them. Acknowledging and being sensitive to his feelings, even while reassuring, soothing, and comforting the client would produce the best result. This would allow him to feel heard, and yet not advance his expression of negative emotions. Confronting a client with a diagnosis of paranoid schizophrenia could easily cause an overreaction and escalation of emotion. Further, feelings of heightened anxiety and/or paranoia could easily grow to the extent that greater intervention could be required. Joining him in his anger could have a similar escalating result. Unless intense anger is coupled with threats, there would be no immediate need to evaluate the client for issues of homicidality or to involve law enforcement.

129. B: The best way to handle the client's expressions of feelings in this type of service is to limit the expression of intense or deep feelings. It should be noted that a client revealing highly personal or sensitive feelings too early on in the therapeutic process can produce a wedge of embarrassment and/or guilt, which can inhibit the therapeutic process and reduce the ability to provide needed services. This can be particularly problematic when: 1) the services are already of a very short-term nature; and 2) where the services provided are very narrow and do not allow for extensive emotional support. Further, if a client precipitously discharges considerable emotion, it can have the effect of over-burdening the social worker/case manager. Thus, the expression of feelings in the therapeutic relationship should: 1) be metered and managed to not outstrip the bonds and ties of the growing relationship; and 2) should be maintained within the scope and mission of the services being provided so as to not leave the client feeling abandoned when services are necessarily terminated.

130. C: If the social worker only has time for one visit, the most critical visit is the 16-year-old girl who was raped because she requires immediate emotional support and assistance. The next visit should be to 14-year-old the boy who attempted suicide because he is at risk for repeat attempts and being hospitalized may be frightening for the adolescent. The third visit should be to the 12-year-old boy who repeatedly runs away to try to determine the reason and to try to mitigate issues if possible. The last visit is to the 2-year-old girl because this is a routine visit.

131. C: The first role of the social worker in these circumstances is to ensure a nonjudgmental attitude, regardless of the client's past. Typically, clients are aware of longstanding societal mores, standards, expectations, and morality. While not always fully aware of the entire scope of the legal ramifications of their choices, most clients know when they are participating in illicit activities. Where an understanding of the consequences of their choices was lacking, by the time they have sought help (or have been mandated to seek it), they are typically well aware of many of the consequences involved. Thus, clients will usually feel averse to the social worker offering a roster of such things in response to their disclosures. Rather, clients are looking to be understood and accepted. Where their behavior is obviously unacceptable, the person should nevertheless be accepted and understood for the pain they are experiencing. Thus, blame, judgment, critique, and other such responses should be withheld and a nonjudgmental attitude should prevail. Where this is not forthcoming, the client will typically sense it, even if not verbalized, and it will hamper the development of a therapeutic bond and the ability to work together positively.

132. C: The proper response would be to meet with administration to address the use of the form. The release of information, particularly information about substance abuse, mental health, and HIV status, is governed by both federal and state laws. Federal HIPAA regulations always apply, and these regulations are not dependent upon an individual's legal standing (incarcerated, on parole or probation, etc.). Minimum standards for a release of information are: 1) the individual's identifying information; 2) identifying information for the recipient of information; 3) the purpose of the release; 4) the specific information to be released (with the client having the right to review the release of specific mental health information prior to authorizing it); and 5) the duration of validity of the signed release (i.e., an expiration date). Other regulations apply in circumstances of imminent danger to the client or others, thus removing the need to circumvent an appropriate form. Both ethics and confidentiality laws are relevant in any release of information.

133. B: Law enforcement personnel are not entitled to confidential client information without a court order, unless there are imminent circumstances of life-threatening danger to the client or others. Valid exclusions to confidentiality include: 1) situations of actively expressed suicidal ideation by the client; 2) when a client leads a social worker to genuinely suspect a client may harm to others (if homicidality is suspected, Tarasoff regulations apply); 3) if a client discloses abuse (physical injury or gross neglect, sexual abuse, etc.) to a minor or a dependent adult; and 4) in situations of grave disability, where a client lacks the mental capacity to secure (or direct others to secure) essential food, clothing, shelter, essential medical care, etc. In all exceptions, the information to be released should be limited to that requisite to resolve the immediate circumstance involved.

134. D: Confidentiality cannot be entirely assured in a group counseling setting; it is no longer just the social worker who is privy to confidential information. Even so, group participants can and should be put under commitment to keep confidential all information shared in group. This should extend to not discussing information about other participants outside group in any way, even among themselves. Further emphasis on confidentiality can be provided by including a confidentiality clause in written treatment consent paperwork. In spite of this, some participants may not manage confidentiality well and all group participants should be apprised of this when entering the group counseling agreement. In this way, participants can be particularly careful about sharing unnecessarily personal information in an open group setting.

135. C: The best response is to request the court withdraw the order, or limit its scope. When possible, psychologically damaging information should be protected from an open court setting. While a social worker may be compelled to testify in certain situations, it is always appropriate to petition the court to withdraw the order by providing a rationale for the concerns involved. Failing this, it remains appropriate to petition the court to limit the scope of the testimony being sought to information that would not be psychologically damaging to the client. While a prosecutor or plaintiff's attorney may attempt to exact as much testimony as possible to press the case more readily to a favorable conclusion, the judge will have no such bias and may agree to withdraw or revise a subpoena if given adequate rationale and insight. The client's mental health should always remain the social worker's first priority, along with honest efforts to maintain agreed upon confidentiality.

136. A: In situations of death, confidentiality agreements remain in full force and effect. Confidentiality agreements are entered into between a client and his or her social worker. They remain legally binding for the two parties involved, even in the event of demise or incapacity. They also remain ethically binding for any new social worker who receives the records of a previous client, and upon the original social worker should his or her client die. To ensure continuity of confidentiality, it is important for social workers to make provisions for their records in the event they die or become cognitively incapacitated. This may involve reciprocal agreements with trusted colleagues or an attorney, or some other appropriate means. Regardless of the provisions made, they should adequately protect a client's confidential information and privacy as fully as possible. Failing to make such provisions constitutes a failure to look after the welfare and well-being of the social worker's clients, and legal action can be taken against a social worker's estate if this is neglected.

137. C: The first step should be to seek supervision and/or consultation. Referring the client to another social worker is a profound disservice to the client. He will be difficult for anyone to work with, and reestablishing with another social worker will be time-consuming and costly. Sharing these feelings with the client will damage the relationship, and will certainly escalate the problem behaviors that have been so troublesome in the first place. Ignoring the problem will not improve it in any way. Clearly these behaviors are very entrenched in the client's interactive repertoire, and thus will continue unless properly addressed and redirected. Engaging in supervision and/or consultation is therefore essential, both for the client's well-being and to produce a therapeutic engagement plan that can be successful. Ongoing consultation and revision of any plan produced will almost certainly be required over time.

138. A: The social worker should first explore the meaning of the gift with the family. Small tokens of appreciation can be graciously accepted, but gifts suffused with deeper meaning (assuming bonding, or symbolizing something that obligates the client to the clinician) should be avoided. When accepting even a small token gift, a clinician should cite ethical standards for the client's future reference. An open and gracious expression of appreciation should always be the response to a small gift. Adding information about ethical standards, however, is important to set the idea of boundaries. It is best, however, to preempt the issue during an intake session, explaining that professional standards prohibit receiving or exchanging gifts. In this way the family becomes aware of guidelines, without encountering a subsequent rejection of a modest gift. If cash or a check in a modest amount is received in the mail from a client or family of ample means, it may be donated to a cause important to the family and in their name (typically a notice of recognition and appreciation is then sent to the family by the organization). Always document any gift situation and resolution in the clinical record so that the outcome is clear.

139. D: The best response is to decline the offer, citing professional ethics. At issue is the creation of a dual relationship, one that extends beyond the clinical setting into other areas of work and life. The social work *Code of Ethics* specifically addresses exploitive relationships, where the social worker holds an undue power advantage. Such relationships should be avoided. For non-exploitive exchanges, there are two views on the matter: the deontological (categorical), calling for total avoidance, and the utilitarian (situational), suggesting a reasoning process. With past clients, the following questions may help: 1) is it exploitive; 2) how much time has passed; 3) the nature (length and intensity) of the relationship; 4) events at termination; 5) the client's vulnerability; 6) the likelihood of a negative impact on the client. A boundary crossing occurs when one bends the code situationally, and boundary violations involve breaking the code. A crossing becomes a clear violation when the dual relationship has negative consequences for the client.

140. C: If the social worker is aware of a quality assurance problem, such as redundant documentation, it is the responsibility of the social worker to take action in a way that is most effective. In this case, the social worker should do a mockup of revised documents and take them to the supervisor because simply complaining or asking the supervisor or other staff to consider revising the documents puts the burden on someone else. When suggesting changes to policies or procedures, it is best to come well-prepared with supporting evidence/samples.

141. C: The most appropriate response would be to attend the funeral, but decline the luncheon invitation. In this situation it is entirely appropriate to accept an invitation to the funeral, demonstrating a show of care and respect for the deceased client and family. For many, it offers an important sense of closure to a loss that the social worker has also experienced. However, the family-only luncheon serves to place the social worker in a more intimate family-like relationship. It can also be a difficult situation for all involved, as gauging appropriate comments and conversation may be challenging among extended family members—a great many of whom will have no relationship with the social worker. Exploring the meaning of the invitation with the family at the time it is extended will allow the social worker to better reassure them and help them understand the important ethical issues involved in stepping out of a preexisting formal role of a counseling nature.

142. A: If the social worker has a 16-year-old morbidly obese client who engages in binge-eating and regains lost weight and feels increasingly worthless because of her failure to lose weight, the first thing the social worker should focus on is the triggers that result in binge eating. The social worker might begin by asking the client to think back to the last episode and discuss what the client was feeling when the client began binging and what might have happened to trigger the desire to binge.

143. A: An example of a leading question would be, "You really do want to go back to school, don't you?" In this way, the client is prompted to agree to something important. However, caution must be used with such questions, as it does not allow for a client's true feelings to necessarily find expression. *Stacked questions* are produced by asking questions in rapid succession, leaving no time for a response and thus shaping the course of the conversation. *Open-ended questions* are constructed to as to elude a "yes" or "no" response, and elicit greater meaning and interpretation (e.g., "How did that make you feel?"). *Close-ended questions* are intended to elicit short and specific answers (e.g., "When were you born?").

144. C: In this situation, the most appropriate therapeutic response would be through confrontation. Empathic Responding refers to accurate perception of a client's feelings followed by accurate restating and sharing. While empathic responding can lead to better therapeutic outcomes, it is not the first-choice technique when a client persists in deluding herself into thinking violating behaviors were simple mistakes or happenings that were sought out by a victim with clear understanding. Reflective (Active) Listening is a useful tool for establishing mutual understandings between individuals. However, it is not designed to identify illicit behavior and directly prompt change. Confrontation can prompt change, though in a rather emotionally traumatic way. Because of this, confrontation must be: 1) carefully timed, usually immediately after the problematic expression or event; 2) with enough time remaining in session to reground the relationship; 3) specific to the issue being addressed; 4) client-focused (as opposed to allowing the social worker to vent at the client's expense); and 5) culturally centered: recognizing how the client will receive the experience, and using an interpreter of there is a language barrier.

145. B: Transference is an emotional reaction toward another, drawn from prior experiences with someone else. For example, feeling resentment toward an employer who seems to treat you in ways reminiscent of how your father treated you. Transference is typically something one remains unaware of without careful thought. It can be a substantial barrier to a therapeutic relationship unless it is addressed and resolved. When a social worker has reactions toward a client based upon the social worker's own background, it is called counter-transference. Other client-based communication barriers include the use of problem minimization or outright denial; reluctance to be honest about something for fear of rejection; limits on open sharing due a fear of losing emotional control; and limits on sharing due to mistrust. Social worker barriers to communication include excessive passivity, leaving the client feeling unsupported; over-aggression, causing the client to feel threatened and unsafe; premature assurance, limiting full disclosure; too much self-disclosure, focusing away from the client; as well as, sarcasm, guilt, judgment, interrupting, and inappropriate humor.

146. A: If a parent appears to have good communication with his child and shows much warmth and affection but imposes few limits, this is typical of permissive parenting. This often results in a child who is creative but has difficulty cooperating with others and may be self-centered and impulsive. The child often has difficulty making friends and may engage in bullying, aggressive, and rebellious behavior. During adolescence, the child may be less mature and less responsible than peers.

147. C: The term journal notes is never used to refer to a social worker's case notes in any way. The *primary client record* is sometimes referred to as the clinical or medical record. The second kind of case notes are referred to as *psychotherapy notes*. In this record the social worker records private notes for subsequent clinical analysis of social worker-client communications. All social worker notes may be more readily subject to subpoena or court-ordered disclosure if they are kept together. However, if kept separately, the private therapy notes are much more difficult to obtain. The primary client record includes information such as assessment, clinical tests, diagnosis, medical information, the treatment plan and treatment modalities used, progress notes, collateral information, billing records, dates and times of sessions, etc. If a subpoena is received requesting the "complete medical record," it need not include the separate psychotherapy notes without further legal stipulation.

148. C: The best response is to seek supervision and/or consultation to explore the issue further. The diagnosis problem cannot be ignored for two important reasons: 1) it leaves the underlying condition untreated, as the client currently receives medications for bipolar disorder and no treatment for the depression and grief issues; and 2) billing under a known erroneous diagnosis can constitute fraud, if it continues. Correcting a diagnosis made by a psychiatrist, however, would not typically be undertaken independently by a social work case manager. Instead, supervision and/or consultation should be obtained to ensure that any attempted corrective steps are not inappropriate, and to ensure that essential services for the client are not terminated without alternative support in place in advance.

149. D: The clients records should next be retained in accordance with state medical record statutes. Not all states have statutes governing the retention period for social work clinical notes. Of those states that do have statutes, the minimum retention period was 3 years and the maximum as much as 10 years. Other standards may apply for clients under the age of majority, who may have further need of the records during their minor years. Where no statutes exist, it has been advised that clinicians retain records in accordance with statutes governing the management of medical records. Regardless, clinicians should be sensitive to the fact that clients may return for further services at a future date, whereupon a prior record could be of considerable assistance in exploring, understanding, and resolving any subsequent problems.

150. A: The best response is to help the family explore their feelings about the defects, their family circumstances, and the meaning of available options. It is essential that the family be permitted to find their own answers in a way that meets their own values and allows them all their rights under the law. Merely offering a dispassionate review of options does not assist the family in discerning their personal and unique feelings about the circumstances. Providing a review of the sanctity of life serves to pressure them into a life-prolonging decision, and emphasizing the reasonable nature of raising a child with even mild defects again pressures them to bear a child in an absence of information that could help them fully understand the meaning and significance of raising that child. If the social worker does not feel able to assist them in fully and personally coming to a decision based on their own values and beliefs, then she should defer to a colleague to provide these important services.

How to Overcome Test Anxiety

Just the thought of taking a test is enough to make most people a little nervous. A test is an important event that can have a long-term impact on your future, so it's important to take it seriously and it's natural to feel anxious about performing well. But just because anxiety is normal, that doesn't mean that it's helpful in test taking, or that you should simply accept it as part of your life. Anxiety can have a variety of effects. These effects can be mild, like making you feel slightly nervous, or severe, like blocking your ability to focus or remember even a simple detail.

If you experience test anxiety—whether severe or mild—it's important to know how to beat it. To discover this, first you need to understand what causes test anxiety.

Causes of Test Anxiety

While we often think of anxiety as an uncontrollable emotional state, it can actually be caused by simple, practical things. One of the most common causes of test anxiety is that a person does not feel adequately prepared for their test. This feeling can be the result of many different issues such as poor study habits or lack of organization, but the most common culprit is time management. Starting to study too late, failing to organize your study time to cover all of the material, or being distracted while you study will mean that you're not well prepared for the test. This may lead to cramming the night before, which will cause you to be physically and mentally exhausted for the test. Poor time management also contributes to feelings of stress, fear, and hopelessness as you realize you are not well prepared but don't know what to do about it.

Other times, test anxiety is not related to your preparation for the test but comes from unresolved fear. This may be a past failure on a test, or poor performance on tests in general. It may come from comparing yourself to others who seem to be performing better or from the stress of living up to expectations. Anxiety may be driven by fears of the future—how failure on this test would affect your educational and career goals. These fears are often completely irrational, but they can still negatively impact your test performance.

> **Review Video: 3 Reasons You Have Test Anxiety**
> Visit mometrix.com/academy and enter code: 428468

Elements of Test Anxiety

As mentioned earlier, test anxiety is considered to be an emotional state, but it has physical and mental components as well. Sometimes you may not even realize that you are suffering from test anxiety until you notice the physical symptoms. These can include trembling hands, rapid heartbeat, sweating, nausea, and tense muscles. Extreme anxiety may lead to fainting or vomiting. Obviously, any of these symptoms can have a negative impact on testing. It is important to recognize them as soon as they begin to occur so that you can address the problem before it damages your performance.

Review Video: 3 Ways to Tell You Have Test Anxiety
Visit mometrix.com/academy and enter code: 927847

The mental components of test anxiety include trouble focusing and inability to remember learned information. During a test, your mind is on high alert, which can help you recall information and stay focused for an extended period of time. However, anxiety interferes with your mind's natural processes, causing you to blank out, even on the questions you know well. The strain of testing during anxiety makes it difficult to stay focused, especially on a test that may take several hours. Extreme anxiety can take a huge mental toll, making it difficult not only to recall test information but even to understand the test questions or pull your thoughts together.

Review Video: How Test Anxiety Affects Memory
Visit mometrix.com/academy and enter code: 609003

Effects of Test Anxiety

Test anxiety is like a disease—if left untreated, it will get progressively worse. Anxiety leads to poor performance, and this reinforces the feelings of fear and failure, which in turn lead to poor performances on subsequent tests. It can grow from a mild nervousness to a crippling condition. If allowed to progress, test anxiety can have a big impact on your schooling, and consequently on your future.

Test anxiety can spread to other parts of your life. Anxiety on tests can become anxiety in any stressful situation, and blanking on a test can turn into panicking in a job situation. But fortunately, you don't have to let anxiety rule your testing and determine your grades. There are a number of relatively simple steps you can take to move past anxiety and function normally on a test and in the rest of life.

Review Video: How Test Anxiety Impacts Your Grades
Visit mometrix.com/academy and enter code: 939819

Physical Steps for Beating Test Anxiety

While test anxiety is a serious problem, the good news is that it can be overcome. It doesn't have to control your ability to think and remember information. While it may take time, you can begin taking steps today to beat anxiety.

Just as your first hint that you may be struggling with anxiety comes from the physical symptoms, the first step to treating it is also physical. Rest is crucial for having a clear, strong mind. If you are tired, it is much easier to give in to anxiety. But if you establish good sleep habits, your body and mind will be ready to perform optimally, without the strain of exhaustion. Additionally, sleeping well helps you to retain information better, so you're more likely to recall the answers when you see the test questions.

Getting good sleep means more than going to bed on time. It's important to allow your brain time to relax. Take study breaks from time to time so it doesn't get overworked, and don't study right before bed. Take time to rest your mind before trying to rest your body, or you may find it difficult to fall asleep.

Review Video: The Importance of Sleep for Your Brain
Visit mometrix.com/academy and enter code: 319338

Along with sleep, other aspects of physical health are important in preparing for a test. Good nutrition is vital for good brain function. Sugary foods and drinks may give a burst of energy but this burst is followed by a crash, both physically and emotionally. Instead, fuel your body with protein and vitamin-rich foods.

Also, drink plenty of water. Dehydration can lead to headaches and exhaustion, especially if your brain is already under stress from the rigors of the test. Particularly if your test is a long one, drink water during the breaks. And if possible, take an energy-boosting snack to eat between sections.

Review Video: How Diet Can Affect your Mood
Visit mometrix.com/academy and enter code: 624317

Along with sleep and diet, a third important part of physical health is exercise. Maintaining a steady workout schedule is helpful, but even taking 5-minute study breaks to walk can help get your blood pumping faster and clear your head. Exercise also releases endorphins, which contribute to a positive feeling and can help combat test anxiety.

When you nurture your physical health, you are also contributing to your mental health. If your body is healthy, your mind is much more likely to be healthy as well. So take time to rest, nourish your body with healthy food and water, and get moving as much as possible. Taking these physical steps will make you stronger and more able to take the mental steps necessary to overcome test anxiety.

Review Video: How to Stay Healthy and Prevent Test Anxiety
Visit mometrix.com/academy and enter code: 877894

Mental Steps for Beating Test Anxiety

Working on the mental side of test anxiety can be more challenging, but as with the physical side, there are clear steps you can take to overcome it. As mentioned earlier, test anxiety often stems from lack of preparation, so the obvious solution is to prepare for the test. Effective studying may be the most important weapon you have for beating test anxiety, but you can and should employ several other mental tools to combat fear.

First, boost your confidence by reminding yourself of past success—tests or projects that you aced. If you're putting as much effort into preparing for this test as you did for those, there's no reason you should expect to fail here. Work hard to prepare; then trust your preparation.

Second, surround yourself with encouraging people. It can be helpful to find a study group, but be sure that the people you're around will encourage a positive attitude. If you spend time with others who are anxious or cynical, this will only contribute to your own anxiety. Look for others who are motivated to study hard from a desire to succeed, not from a fear of failure.

Third, reward yourself. A test is physically and mentally tiring, even without anxiety, and it can be helpful to have something to look forward to. Plan an activity following the test, regardless of the outcome, such as going to a movie or getting ice cream.

When you are taking the test, if you find yourself beginning to feel anxious, remind yourself that you know the material. Visualize successfully completing the test. Then take a few deep, relaxing breaths and return to it. Work through the questions carefully but with confidence, knowing that you are capable of succeeding.

Developing a healthy mental approach to test taking will also aid in other areas of life. Test anxiety affects more than just the actual test—it can be damaging to your mental health and even contribute to depression. It's important to beat test anxiety before it becomes a problem for more than testing.

Review Video: <u>Test Anxiety and Depression</u>
Visit mometrix.com/academy and enter code: 904704

Study Strategy

Being prepared for the test is necessary to combat anxiety, but what does being prepared look like? You may study for hours on end and still not feel prepared. What you need is a strategy for test prep. The next few pages outline our recommended steps to help you plan out and conquer the challenge of preparation.

STEP 1: SCOPE OUT THE TEST

Learn everything you can about the format (multiple choice, essay, etc.) and what will be on the test. Gather any study materials, course outlines, or sample exams that may be available. Not only will this help you to prepare, but knowing what to expect can help to alleviate test anxiety.

STEP 2: MAP OUT THE MATERIAL

Look through the textbook or study guide and make note of how many chapters or sections it has. Then divide these over the time you have. For example, if a book has 15 chapters and you have five days to study, you need to cover three chapters each day. Even better, if you have the time, leave an extra day at the end for overall review after you have gone through the material in depth.

If time is limited, you may need to prioritize the material. Look through it and make note of which sections you think you already have a good grasp on, and which need review. While you are studying, skim quickly through the familiar sections and take more time on the challenging parts. Write out your plan so you don't get lost as you go. Having a written plan also helps you feel more in control of the study, so anxiety is less likely to arise from feeling overwhelmed at the amount to cover.

STEP 3: GATHER YOUR TOOLS

Decide what study method works best for you. Do you prefer to highlight in the book as you study and then go back over the highlighted portions? Or do you type out notes of the important information? Or is it helpful to make flashcards that you can carry with you? Assemble the pens, index cards, highlighters, post-it notes, and any other materials you may need so you won't be distracted by getting up to find things while you study.

If you're having a hard time retaining the information or organizing your notes, experiment with different methods. For example, try color-coding by subject with colored pens, highlighters, or post-it notes. If you learn better by hearing, try recording yourself reading your notes so you can listen while in the car, working out, or simply sitting at your desk. Ask a friend to quiz you from your flashcards, or try teaching someone the material to solidify it in your mind.

STEP 4: CREATE YOUR ENVIRONMENT

It's important to avoid distractions while you study. This includes both the obvious distractions like visitors and the subtle distractions like an uncomfortable chair (or a too-comfortable couch that makes you want to fall asleep). Set up the best study environment possible: good lighting and a comfortable work area. If background music helps you focus, you may want to turn it on, but otherwise keep the room quiet. If you are using a computer to take notes, be sure you don't have any other windows open, especially applications like social media, games, or anything else that could distract you. Silence your phone and turn off notifications. Be sure to keep water close by so you stay hydrated while you study (but avoid unhealthy drinks and snacks).

Also, take into account the best time of day to study. Are you freshest first thing in the morning? Try to set aside some time then to work through the material. Is your mind clearer in the afternoon or evening? Schedule your study session then. Another method is to study at the same time of day that you will take the test, so that your brain gets used to working on the material at that time and will be ready to focus at test time.

STEP 5: STUDY!

Once you have done all the study preparation, it's time to settle into the actual studying. Sit down, take a few moments to settle your mind so you can focus, and begin to follow your study plan. Don't give in to distractions or let yourself procrastinate. This is your time to prepare so you'll be ready to fearlessly approach the test. Make the most of the time and stay focused.

Of course, you don't want to burn out. If you study too long you may find that you're not retaining the information very well. Take regular study breaks. For example, taking five minutes out of every hour to walk briskly, breathing deeply and swinging your arms, can help your mind stay fresh.

As you get to the end of each chapter or section, it's a good idea to do a quick review. Remind yourself of what you learned and work on any difficult parts. When you feel that you've mastered the material, move on to the next part. At the end of your study session, briefly skim through your notes again.

But while review is helpful, cramming last minute is NOT. If at all possible, work ahead so that you won't need to fit all your study into the last day. Cramming overloads your brain with more information than it can process and retain, and your tired mind may struggle to recall even previously learned information when it is overwhelmed with last-minute study. Also, the urgent nature of cramming and the stress placed on your brain contribute to anxiety. You'll be more likely to go to the test feeling unprepared and having trouble thinking clearly.

So don't cram, and don't stay up late before the test, even just to review your notes at a leisurely pace. Your brain needs rest more than it needs to go over the information again. In fact, plan to finish your studies by noon or early afternoon the day before the test. Give your brain the rest of the day to relax or focus on other things, and get a good night's sleep. Then you will be fresh for the test and better able to recall what you've studied.

STEP 6: TAKE A PRACTICE TEST

Many courses offer sample tests, either online or in the study materials. This is an excellent resource to check whether you have mastered the material, as well as to prepare for the test format and environment.

Check the test format ahead of time: the number of questions, the type (multiple choice, free response, etc.), and the time limit. Then create a plan for working through them. For example, if you have 30 minutes to take a 60-question test, your limit is 30 seconds per question. Spend less time on the questions you know well so that you can take more time on the difficult ones.

If you have time to take several practice tests, take the first one open book, with no time limit. Work through the questions at your own pace and make sure you fully understand them. Gradually work up to taking a test under test conditions: sit at a desk with all study materials put away and set a timer. Pace yourself to make sure you finish the test with time to spare and go back to check your answers if you have time.

After each test, check your answers. On the questions you missed, be sure you understand why you missed them. Did you misread the question (tests can use tricky wording)? Did you forget the information? Or was it something you hadn't learned? Go back and study any shaky areas that the practice tests reveal.

Taking these tests not only helps with your grade, but also aids in combating test anxiety. If you're already used to the test conditions, you're less likely to worry about it, and working through tests until you're scoring well gives you a confidence boost. Go through the practice tests until you feel comfortable, and then you can go into the test knowing that you're ready for it.

Test Tips

On test day, you should be confident, knowing that you've prepared well and are ready to answer the questions. But aside from preparation, there are several test day strategies you can employ to maximize your performance.

First, as stated before, get a good night's sleep the night before the test (and for several nights before that, if possible). Go into the test with a fresh, alert mind rather than staying up late to study.

Try not to change too much about your normal routine on the day of the test. It's important to eat a nutritious breakfast, but if you normally don't eat breakfast at all, consider eating just a protein bar. If you're a coffee drinker, go ahead and have your normal coffee. Just make sure you time it so that the caffeine doesn't wear off right in the middle of your test. Avoid sugary beverages, and drink enough water to stay hydrated but not so much that you need a restroom break 10 minutes into the test. If your test isn't first thing in the morning, consider going for a walk or doing a light workout before the test to get your blood flowing.

Allow yourself enough time to get ready, and leave for the test with plenty of time to spare so you won't have the anxiety of scrambling to arrive in time. Another reason to be early is to select a good seat. It's helpful to sit away from doors and windows, which can be distracting. Find a good seat, get out your supplies, and settle your mind before the test begins.

When the test begins, start by going over the instructions carefully, even if you already know what to expect. Make sure you avoid any careless mistakes by following the directions.

Then begin working through the questions, pacing yourself as you've practiced. If you're not sure on an answer, don't spend too much time on it, and don't let it shake your confidence. Either skip it and come back later, or eliminate as many wrong answers as possible and guess among the remaining ones. Don't dwell on these questions as you continue—put them out of your mind and focus on what lies ahead.

Be sure to read all of the answer choices, even if you're sure the first one is the right answer. Sometimes you'll find a better one if you keep reading. But don't second-guess yourself if you do immediately know the answer. Your gut instinct is usually right. Don't let test anxiety rob you of the information you know.

If you have time at the end of the test (and if the test format allows), go back and review your answers. Be cautious about changing any, since your first instinct tends to be correct, but make sure you didn't misread any of the questions or accidentally mark the wrong answer choice. Look over any you skipped and make an educated guess.

At the end, leave the test feeling confident. You've done your best, so don't waste time worrying about your performance or wishing you could change anything. Instead, celebrate the successful

completion of this test. And finally, use this test to learn how to deal with anxiety even better next time.

Important Qualification

Not all anxiety is created equal. If your test anxiety is causing major issues in your life beyond the classroom or testing center, or if you are experiencing troubling physical symptoms related to your anxiety, it may be a sign of a serious physiological or psychological condition. If this sounds like your situation, we strongly encourage you to seek professional help.

Thank You

We at Mometrix would like to extend our heartfelt thanks to you, our friend and patron, for allowing us to play a part in your journey. It is a privilege to serve people from all walks of life who are unified in their commitment to building the best future they can for themselves.

The preparation you devote to these important testing milestones may be the most valuable educational opportunity you have for making a real difference in your life. We encourage you to put your heart into it—that feeling of succeeding, overcoming, and yes, conquering will be well worth the hours you've invested.

We want to hear your story, your struggles and your successes, and if you see any opportunities for us to improve our materials so we can help others even more effectively in the future, please share that with us as well. **The team at Mometrix would be absolutely thrilled to hear from you!** So please, send us an email (support@mometrix.com) and let's stay in touch.

If you'd like some additional help, check out these other resources we offer for your exam:
http://mometrixflashcards.com/ASWB